DISCONTENT AND DANGER IN INDIA

DISCONTENT AND DANGER IN INDIA

A. K. CONNEL

GYAN

Published by

GYAN

Gyan Publishing House
5, Ansari Road
Daryaganj, New Delhi-110002
Phone: 011-47034999, 9811692060
E-mail: books@gyanbooks.com

Distribution Network
gyanbooks.com
India, USA, Canada, UK, Australia

ISBN: 978-93-7133-088-6 (PB)

First Published, 1880

2nd Impression 2026

Printed at: Gyan Press, Delhi.

DISCONTENT AND DANGER IN INDIA

Author: A. K. CONNEL

DISCONTENT AND DANGER IN INDIA

DISCONTENT AND DANGER IN INDIA

BY

A. K. CONNELL, M.A.

LATE SCHOLAR OF NEW COLLEGE, OXFORD

LONDON

C. KEGAN PAUL & CO., 1 PATERNOSTER SQUARE

1880

'The temper of the people, amongst whom he presides, ought to be the first study of a statesman.'—BURKE.

'οἱ μέν γε νεωτεροποιοὶ καὶ ἐπινοῆσαι ὀξεῖς καὶ ἐπιτελέσαι ἔργῳ ἃ ἂν γνῶσιν, οἱ δὲ τὰ ὑπάρχοντά τε σῴζειν καὶ ἐπιγνῶναι μηδὲν καὶ ἔργῳ οὐδὲ τἀναγκαῖα ἐξικέσθαι.'—THUCYDIDES.

'As a rule, a stationary state is by far the most frequent condition of man, as far as history describes that condition; the progressive state is only a rare and an occasional exception.'

BAGEHOT.

'Alle Verhältnisse zwischen den Einzeln haben nur Werth, sofern sie Verhältnisse zwischen bewussten Wesen sind, und eben deswegen nicht blos *zwischen* ihnen im Leeren, sondern auch *in* ihnen bestehen, in dem lebendigen Gemüth ihrem Werthe nach gefühlt und genossen werden.'—LOTZE.

PREFACE.

IN ORDER to show that I have not ventured without due preparation to envisage the complex problems presented by our Indian Empire, I must mention a few personal details. I was in Northern India from March 1879–80, and having during that time complete leisure, and being for some months at one of the centres of Administration, I took the opportunity of gaining as much insight as possible into the mysteries of our Indian bureaucracy. I devoured and in part digested the *pabulum* provided so lavishly by the Governmental presses in the shape of Gazettes, Famine, Settlement, Administration, and Deccan Riots Reports, &c.; but the opinions of experienced Anglo-Indians with whom I came in contact, and whom I mercilessly button-holed, were a more invaluable source of information. In spite of special obligations I intend to mention no names, as a Government conducted on strictly confidential principles does not like *its* servants (they are of course in India not the public's servants) to talk freely about its private affairs. Perhaps I am generalising too hastily from the sacrosanct secrecy of the late *régime*, when, as we now know, nine crores of rupees, taking advantage of official reticence and financial superabundance, calmly walked away; but I think it best to take the safe side.

I may add that being out in camp during the cold weather, in an ordinary rural district, I had the —for an outsider—unusual opportunity of seeing how the administrative machinery works and affects the native's daily life.

As some set-off against my gloomy tone, I feel bound to express my deep admiration for the hard-worked district officers, whether civil or military, who are the true pillars of the British Empire. Separated for months, if not for years, from wives and children, deprived of any congenial society for the greater part of the cold weather, struggling against *ennui* during the hot weather (they do not, like some great officials, receive travelling allowances to go to the hills, after being paid high salaries to stay in the plains), plagued in the performance of their proper duties by needless paper work, these men have in mind and body to bear the burden and heat of the day. They may not receive any mark of approval, they may lie in 'unvisited tombs'; but if there is any virtue, if there is any strength, in our Indian Empire, it is *their* self-sacrificing zeal, *their* courageous and independent spirit, that has called it into being. 'Verily they have their reward'—not, it may be, in the plaudits of their countrymen, but in the deep gratitude of an alien people, whose childlike emotions they have touched by their fatherly care. To those among them whom I am proud to call my friends, I dedicate this book, in the hope that their protests may reach a wider and more powerful audience, and that they may not be invalidated by any shortcomings on my part. If I succeed in enlightening those who already take a real interest in the welfare of India, and in adding to their number, I hall not consider my labour misspent.

LONDON: *July* 1880.

CONTENTS.

APPENDIX I.

APPENDIX II.

APPENDIX III.

APPENDIX IV.

APPENDIX V.

APPENDIX VI.

APPENDIX VII.

APPENDIX VIII.

APPENDIX IX.

APPENDIX X.

APPENDIX XI.

APPENDIX XII.

DISCONTENT AND DANGER IN INDIA.

CHAPTER I.

THERE is a grim irony in the destiny which, after centuries of separation, has led the most energetic portion of the Aryan family, especially characterised by the intensity of its national spirit and the freedom of its political life, to undertake the government of the most stationary portion of the same family, still further retarded by the absorption of alien and less advanced races, and sharply differentiated from its rulers by the non-development of any political idea beyond that of the strong man armed. And yet this striking contrast, with all its far-reaching consequences, has hitherto been insisted upon with but little emphasis by writers who have undertaken to enlighten the British public on Indian affairs, and the fact of its existence tends to be lost sight of even by statesmen who preside at the India Office.

It is only quite recently that the question, What

are the economical, social, and moral results of British rule in India? has received the attention of the non-official world, and that public opinion in England has begun to bring independent criticism to bear on the weighty problems which have to be faced in our great dependency. It is true that Blue-books on the material and moral progress—as it is complacently assumed to be—of India are made up year by year from official sources, and a pleasant picture, based on statistics, is presented for the admiration of the outside world. But such cheerful confidence will fail to reassure anyone who has had the opportunity of studying the question on the spot, supplementing official reports by the oral testimony of district officers, who are most in contact with the people, and who have not allowed their eyesight to grow dim beneath the glamour of bureaucratic optimism.

Nor is it at all surprising that our Indian Empire should suggest very painful considerations when we remember the teasing procedure with which it is synonymous. The Socratic method, which was found rather irksome when worked over a limited area by a single enthusiast, is there applied on a much wider scale, and through the agency of an organised mission. Moreover, the vigour of the method has greatly increased. For while at Athens the Greek philosopher, to borrow the well-known metaphor of Plato, confined himself to bringing to the birth, by persuasive arts, the innate ideas of his fellow-countrymen, in India a clique of Englishmen forces, at the point of the bayonet, its own mature conceptions on a vast and varied population of strangers. The fat babies of the bureaucratic nursery are thrust on their ill-fed foster-parents, who find to their cost that they have harboured wolves which tear and rend their bosoms. They naturally begin to sigh for the more capricious, but less relentless persecution of native despotism, whose hard features are softened by time, and seem less ugly in comparison with those of their present and persistent plague :

> ἄμαχον ἄλγος οἰκέταις
> μέγα σίνος πολυκτόνδον.

This *vexatio naturæ* seems to be the inevitable consequence of the way in which the administration of India is conducted. The Viceroy being sent out for only a few years, is naturally tempted to signalise his short term of office by some measure which will strike the minds of the English public. Indeed, he is induced, by his very position, to regard himself as the bearer of a political evangel, to be forced at all hazards on heathenish Orientals, who are regarded as perishing from the absence of the glad news of Western progress. Each Viceroy is eager to throw all his ability into some policy of unmasterly activity, and it is only now and then that a statesman like Lord Northbrook is content to give the country its much-required interval of repose.

As a rule, the last quarter of a century has been characterised by incessant activity in legislation, just as the previous quarter of a century was marked by incessant activity in annexation. The era of codes has succeeded that of conquests; if the Commander-in-Chief has slain his thousands, the Legal Member of Council has slain his ten thousands.

It might be supposed that this restless energy, if proved prejudicial to the best interests of the country, would have been immediately checked by the Viceroy's Council as a whole. But it must be remembered that three of its number need not have had any Indian experience, and, like the Viceroy, are keen to do something; while the Anglo-Indian members, if inclined to act as checkstrings (sometimes a Sir J. Strachey out-herods Herod), are hardly independent enough for the purpose. As Sir George Campbell pointed out in one of last year's debates on India, 'in old days members of Council received a higher salary than any Deputy or Lieutenant-Governor, and there was no promotion for members of the Council. They were men over whom the Governor-General had no control whatever. Nowadays, the members of the Council receive less salary, and there are very considerable posts in the gift of the Governor-General which are more highly paid than a membership of Council, and to which the members of the Council look for promotion. That has to a considerable degree undermined their independence.' The same opinions were expressed some years ago by Colonel Chesney in his 'Indian Polity,' and he suggested that this defect in the Viceroy's Council would be obviated either by placing the Councillors on the same footing as the Lieutenant-Governors, or by a special enactment declaring them ineligible for further advancement in India. As it is, there is always great danger of the initiation of impolitic action by the least experienced element, and of the remonstrances of local Governments being set aside.

But when, as was too often the case under the late *régime* of rhetoric, the Viceroy is contented with giving literary finish to the bald decrees of a masterful Marquis, the interests of India are likely to be still further sacrificed to the exigencies of party politics. Thus, the inevitable tendency of a foreign Government to disregard the wishes of the governed is abnormally accelerated, and the rule of the foreigner becomes still more abhorrent to every thoughtful native.

And, even under the most favourable circumstances, 'the first study of a statesman' tends to be neglected by the Indian Government, unchecked as it is by any representative system, and unenlightened by any adequate expression of public opinion.* Hence, the normal state of things produces

* It is hardly necessary to point out, if the fact were not so often ignored, the enormous difference between a foreign and indigenous

much irritation. A succession of Socratic gadflies, with stings sharpened by the inherited activities of Western life, have been let loose on the sluggish and somnolent beast of the East, enervated by climate and hampered by custom; and it is not to be wondered at, if the quickening of the latter's paces under incessant goadings leads to very unexpected results.

But, besides the strong impulse to 'go ahead,' which emanates from the highest quarters, there is a perpetual desire in the central secretariat staff to get the maximum of uniformity in administrative machinery—to assimilate all the provinces to the orthodox regulation type, irrespective of their different requirements. Thus it will very often be found that men who, from having passed a great part of their official career away from district work, have lost touch of the people, manage to override the protests of the much more experienced district officers. With complacent dogmatism they deal out their yards of red tape as swaddling-clothes for

despotism. The latter is always tempered by public opinion finding utterance through court officials and the like, and is sometimes, as was seen recently in the case of Russia, absolutely dominated by popular forces. The former is by its very nature cut off from free and friendly intercourse with its subjects, and relies on the strength of its body-guard to carry through its unpopular measures. It is the opinion of the best authorities that there is much less friendliness between the English and the natives of India than there used to be, in great measure owing to the importation of English home-life, the continual shifting of officers from district to district, the memories of the mutiny, and direct taxation. (See Appendix I.)

the ill-clad native, and treat the inhabitants of a country, distinguished above all Orientals for intense conservatism, as so much plastic material to be moulded at their will. Hence come endless acts and rules, gigantic codification schemes, whimsical plans for direct taxation, the costly extravagance of so-called* 'ordinary' public works, and all the other outrageous proposals of reforming administrators, utterly unsuited to India, but imported wholesale from Europe, as the latest results of Western science, whether legal, financial, or engineering.

Such being the outcome of a highly refined bureaucracy, where is the poor vile body which is made the subject of so many experiments to look for help?

It might be thought that Parliament is the true guardian of the permanent interests of India. But it cannot be said that it has hitherto proved adequate to this work. In fact, it really requires itself to be controlled. As J. S. Mill has truly remarked,

* If all the money wasted during the last twenty-five years under this head were to be correctly summed up, the result would be appalling. The Department of Public Works seems to think that it merely exists to spend. The case of the Saugor barracks, which were built only to tumble down, is typical of what has taken place all over India. The cutting down of bloated D. P. W.'s establishments has been one of the wisest measures of retrenchment, although necessitated by the Afghan War. I have heard of a civilian who once attempted to make a list of the D. P. W.'s iniquities, but he gave it up in despair at the amount. Parliament ought to ask for evidence on this matter from district officers.

'the government of a people by itself has a meaning and a reality; but such a thing as government of one people by another does not and cannot exist. One people may keep another as a warren or preserve for its own use, a place to make money in, a human cattle farm to be worked for the profit of its own inhabitants; but if the good of the governed is the proper business of a Government, it is utterly impossible that a people should directly attend to it.' If this was true even when the East India Company was powerful in the House of Commons, and the directors had a legal status in the Queen's Bench, *à fortiori* is it true when the counterbalance to the sinister bias of Parliament has been taken away.

Moreover, even in cases where the British Parliament is moved by the highest motives, the influence of philanthropic fuss sometimes leads it to encourage unwise outlay. The only useful part which, according to J. S. Mill, such an assembly can play, is to ensure publicity and discussion whenever the doings of the British rulers are called in question. 'The utility of such action does not require that the public at large should comprehend the point at issue, provided that there are any individuals who do; the approbation or disapprobation of one person well versed in the subject may outweigh that of the thousands who know nothing at all about it.' He also points out that the Secretary of State must necessarily be influenced by English politics; he seldom is in office long enough to acquire an intelligent interest in such a complicated subject as India; and, it may be added, if he is an able but arrogant man, he may wish to distinguish himself by disdainfully overruling the opinions of experienced Anglo-Indians.

It is therefore obvious that a thoroughly independent body of men, not likely to be swayed by the currents of English politics, is required to stand forth as the staunch champion, not only of the permanent interests of India as a whole against the transient needs of Party Government, but also of the interests of the different provinces, which make up that vast dependency, against the continuous assaults of the Central Government. That this body should be strong and able to assert its authority becomes all the more necessary at the present time, when the centre of authority is getting more and more shifted from Calcutta to London, and the viceregal Council is less independent than it used to be.

To the eye of Lord Cranbrook, surveying the East from the specular heights of the Crystal Palace, India may look like one country made up of one homogeneous nationality; but, as Sir Henry Maine has remarked in his first lecture on 'Village Communities,' 'the apparent uniformity and even monotony which to the new comer are its most impressive characteristics, prove, on larger experience, to have been merely the cloudy outline produced by mental distance; and the observation of each succeeding year discloses a greater variety in usages and ideas which at first seemed everywhere identical.' Indeed, nothing is so incorrect as to confound in one category the Bengali Baboo with his veneer of Western culture, the effect of more than a century of British rule on a facile race; the proud but unlettered Rajpoot and unreceptive Sikh of Northern India, still for the most part untainted by Western ideas, and clinging to the memories of the historic past; and the hardy but semi-savage hill-man of the mountain ranges, or the aboriginal jungle tribesman of Central India and Burmah, but recently reclaimed from an almost animal existence.

It is these strongly-marked differences that make it so important that the utmost deference should be shown to the opinions of the local authorities well acquainted with the conditions of their respective districts. Otherwise the friction which is the inevitable concomitant of British rule is enormously increased; and while so-called administrative reforms are carried out, the people grow more and more estranged, and cling with the tenacity of dying men to those very prejudices whose outward expression in action it is thought desirable to correct. Improvident marriages and extravagant feasts become more precious customs.

There are, obviously, some practices which no Power pretending to any degree of civilisation can possibly tolerate. Life and property must be made secure; suttee, child-murder, and human sacrifices must be suppressed. But in other more indifferent matters the higher ranks of Anglo-Indian officials might learn something—*fas est et ab hoste doceri*—from the way in which Russia has dealt with a similar problem in Central Asia. Although the vicious aspects of Russian rule, such as the corruption of officials and the like, cannot be too strongly reprobated, yet a moderate imitation of her *laisser faire* system, in dealing with native customs, might beneficially modify the strenuous action which has introduced such revolutionary changes into the fabric of the life and thought of the natives of India.

'The experience of the English in India,' writes the late W. Bagehot, 'shows, if it shows anything, that a highly civilised race may fail in producing a rapidly excellent effect on a less civilised race, because it is too good and too excellent. The two are not *en rapport* together; the merits of the one are not the merits prized by the other; the manner-language of the one is not the manner-language of the other. The higher being is not, and cannot be, a model for the lower; he could not mould himself on it if he would, and would not if he could. Consequently the two races have long lived together, "near and yet far off," daily seeing one another and daily interchanging superficial thoughts, but in the depths of their mind separated by a whole era of civilisation, and so affecting one another only a little in comparison with what might have been hoped.' In short, a Government may be too enlightened for a people, and thereby actually retard its progress; and this is necessarily the danger which must attend the steps of an administration conducted by foreigners, characterised by devout belief in the universal applicability of home-grown institutions.

England, with all its free activities, has taken centuries to evolve its present administrative apparatus. Is India, with its deeply-rooted prejudices, to be fitted out with the same apparatus, introduced *ab extra* in less than a century? A legal system, based upon the most advanced ideas of individual rights, and the equality of all men, and worked with stringent penalties in accordance with the scientific ideas of Bentham and Austin, is suddenly imposed on a people whose conception of right is collective rather than personal, and who have till recently been content with the simple coercion of village customs, tempered by occasional anarchy and continual apathy.

The scheme for an uniform Civil Code, lately announced by Mr. Whitley Stokes, dealing among other subjects with such matters as alluvion and diluvion, easements, torts, and the like, as regards which customs vary indefinitely, is only an exaggerated instance of methods of procedure which have been the usual attendants of British rule in

India, and have done so much to spread general irritation.

A native, when once asked by Mr. R. H. Elliot, 'the Mysore planter,'* what he thought of our Government, replied that it was like a monkey, always jumping in an eccentric way. This well expresses the feeling with which many of the feats of a grave officialdom must be regarded by lowly spectators; though the monkeys, no doubt, do not think their movements at all strange, but rather as the pleasing and playful outcome of scientifically developed muscles.

When the history of India during the last twenty years of our rule comes to be written, the reader will be astonished at the perfect plague of laws which has swept over the country.

> Es erben sich Gesetz' und Rechte
> Wie ein' ewige Krankheit fort.

And truly might the cynical native critic add—

> Vom Rechte das mit uns geboren ist,
> Von dem ist, leider! nie die Frage.

No doubt the substitution of a foreign Government based on law for an indigenous one based on personal will has to some extent necessitated the change from unwritten and expansive customs to

* Planters probably know more about the real feelings and thoughts of the natives than any Government official. The latter i always suspected of having an ulterior motive in asking questions, especially when license-taxes, &c., are in vogue. The harm done by such taxes in stopping friendly relations between a district officer and the native is infinite.

written and stereotyped codes; but the very fact that such a process has proved inevitable, and that the act of translation constitutes in itself a gigantic revolution, makes it all the more incumbent on the Indian Government to limit it to what is absolutely necessary, and to discourage 'speculative legislation' like that which is now in vogue. It is too often forgotten that it is men and not machines that have to be set in motion, and that legal rights require popular recognition before they can be truly said to exist. Otherwise they remain *in vacuo*, unsanctioned by that which can alone give them true sanction—the general consciousness of their social helpfulness.

If the inhabitant of that law-flooded land had not erected his social dams in the shape of caste customs, whereby he has been able to stem the inroads of Christian vigour as well as of Mahommedan violence, it is difficult to see how he could have prevented himself from retrograding into a semi-animal existence. A perpetual flux in the whole structure of human relations is not the best social medium for the realisation of higher possibilities; and yet this would have been the inevitable result, without the powers of resistance residing in caste prejudices.

Caste morality may not be high according to Western ideas, but it is the outcome of the efforts of many generations to withstand outward pressure; it is stamped as the work of man, not of nature; it has strong external sanctions; it may move on a low level, but it is effectual within its limits. Any successful assault on it might lead to chaos, not to a better cosmos. Higher life must be developed from the influence of higher ideas. To force a number of reforms on a people whose ideas are not adequate to them, is the sure way of preventing that desired reformation of thought and feeling from which such reforms might ultimately receive vital heat, so as to become part of the living social organism, and without which they remain mere strait-waistcoats, cramping the natural play of the limbs.

Was man nicht nützt, ist eine schwere Last.

To deliver even an indirect attack by legislative enactments on highly-treasured usages must necessarily excite grave discontent.

To the eye of the Legal Member of Council, exhilarated by the cool breezes of the Himalayas, and utterly unacquainted with ordinary country life, the worker in the plains may seem a poor benighted creature, whose clogged condition must be purged by the drastic doses of law. But has not the Hindoo, has not the Mahommedan 'eyes? Hath he not hands, organs, dimensions, senses, affections, passions? If he is pricked, does he not bleed? if he is tickled, does he not laugh? if he is poisoned, does he not die? if he is wronged, will he not revenge?' Alas! profound belief in bureaux and bayonets seems to have a very blinding effect, and the answer is too often in the negative.

CHAPTER II.

DR. HUNTER, in his Edinburgh lectures on 'India,' drew a fascinating picture of the results of British rule, as they appear to the optimistic official mind. He described the many miles of railway which, contemptuous of meandering rivers and mountain ranges, connect the most distant parts of the peninsula, the opening of fresh markets, the rise of cities from malarious swamps, the introduction of new crops, the growth of municipal institutions, the security against violence within and without.

But while this panorama of progress passed before his vision, he somehow failed to inform his audience of the economic and social effect of these great works on the silent myriads. 'Here is everything advantageous to life,' says India's Gonzalo; but ought Antonio's reply, 'True; save the means to live,' to be wholly ignored? Are the masses, in whose interest the administration of India is professedly conducted, as well fed and clothed, as prosperous and happy (there are many more of them), as they were under the best native rule? There is no attempt to deny that the upper classes have lost many privileges which they possessed before, but has the curtailment of their power improved the lot of those beneath them? Does the country, as a whole, receive some compensation for the admittedly costly and uncongenial rule of the foreigner? These are the all-important questions for the English public to ask themselves, and they are not answered by that lucid description of material changes with which the Director-General of Statistics flattered the national pride of the North.

Unconvinced by the glowing apology made by this eloquent hierophant, Mr. Forster, in a speech at Leeds, called attention to the fact that, in spite of the expenditure of millions of pounds sterling* within the last few years, some millions of human beings, not to mention millions of cattle, had died of famine; and he naturally asked for some explanation of this terrible waste of life. Granted that want or excess of rain is the primary cause, the question still remains, whether the distress which inevitably results from scarcity of food-supply is intensified by the action of our administrative system. Does the increase of brain-power on the part of the governors tend to empty the bellies of the governed, and so-called improvements bring in their train general distress, discontent, and de-

* The expenditure on famine during the last ten years is stated in this year's Indian Budget to be £14,607,000. The Famine Commissioners' Report recently issued says that five millions of persons died in the recent famine.

moralisation? No unbiassed inquirer can doubt that there is a reverse side to the shield, the outer surface of which Dr. Hunter burnished to such intense brilliancy; and it is to this dimmer side that it is most necessary to call attention.

As by far the larger portion of the population of India is agricultural, and as a sum of about £21,000,000* is raised directly from the land, it is obvious that the land-revenue system is the most important feature of British administration; yet it is the economic and social effects of this system that have as yet received little attention in England, although there is considerable consensus of opinion on the matter among Anglo-Indian officers, who have had to superintend the fixation and collection of the land-tax.

In Northern India, the Central Provinces, and Bombay, as is well-known, the land revenue is settled for periods of thirty years. In all these divisions of India, with the exception of Bombay, where the agreement to pay the land-tax is made directly with the peasant proprietor cultivating the soil, and where there is no rent in the usual sense of the word to be taken as a guide, the revenue demand is nominally arranged to consist of 50 per cent. of the rental—deductions being allowed in the

* During the last few years it has been to about £22,000,000, but the receipts have been swollen by the arrears of the famine-time. According to the Famine Commissioners' Report, the rural population is 176 millions out of 190 millions. But much of the so-called town population is made up of agriculturists.

case of land which is worked by the proprietor as a home-farm—and is collected in two or more cash instalments from the proprietors,* whether individuals or coparcenary bodies, the latter being represented by their head men.

In Bombay the State claims that surplus portion, paid in cash, of the total produce which it considers—in view of the prices that have prevailed during a certain number of years, allowance being made for difference of soils, and varying advantages, such as communications, &c.—each cultivator will be able to pay in an average year, with a fair margin over for comfort.

* The 50 per cent. assessment is regarded as low, if it is strictly adhered to. It used to be 66 per cent. in the North-Western Provinces before the last settlement, but this was found to be too heavy. The share taken by native rulers is supposed to have been nominally heavier, but it varied a good deal according to the harvests. Its collection could be easily resisted, if necessary. One of the great changes made by the English Government is the universal substitution of cash payments for those in kind, which, under native rule, were very common. What the State takes from the landowner the latter takes from the tenant. As every tenant is forced to sell part of his crop to the grain-dealer at certain fixed seasons in order to pay his rent, he does not make so much by high prices as might be expected. The market gets glutted with grain, while the demand for rupees is increased. Moreover, it must never be forgotten that high prices do not benefit the cultivator as regards that part of his grain which he retains for his own consumption and for seed—a very considerable share of the gross produce. In Bombay, even the pasture-land has to pay a tax; this has seriously affected the number of cattle, according to the Deccan Commission's Report (page 42). The great rise in the price of land is not necessarily the result of its increased yield, but is due partly to greater competition, partly to its saleability, which hardly existed under native rule.

The idea embodied in a thirty years' settlement, is that, on the one hand, by fixing the State's share for a long period, every encouragement will be given to agricultural enterprise; while, by taking a moderate though fixed share of the rent or surplus produce,* the good years ought to cover the bad; and that, on the other hand, the State will not be deprived of its share in the increased value of the soil.

This seems most excellent in theory; but it cannot be said that the practical results have been as beneficial to the agricultural classes as might have been expected. In provinces such as the North-West, where rent is taken as the basis for deciding the State's share, the settlement-officer, influenced by various causes, such as the pressure put on him to fix as large an assessment as possible, or idiosyncrasies as to the present or future value of certain soils, or lastly the difficulty of finding out what is the rent actually paid,† has, in many cases, fixed the

* It is very difficult to say what is the relation of the State's demand to the total produce of the soil. It is generally supposed to be one-sixth, but many authorities would put it at something between one-sixth and one-twelfth of an average yield. Where there is an intermediate class of landowners, the rent is shared equally between the State and the landowners. Where, as in Bombay and Madras, there is no intermediate class, the State theoretically divides that part of the produce which represents rent between itself and the cultivating proprietor. But in Bombay the latter nearly always employs the money-lender as a go-between.

† Where there are what are called occupancy-tenants, with the right of holding at favourable rents, their rents are entered into the village rent-rolls, but in the case of tenants-at-will it is not so easy to find out what they are paying.

State's demand at much more than 50 per cent. of actual assets, and the sudden enhancement has allowed the small landowner no time to readjust himself to his changed circumstances. The result is that the latter is either forced, where he lets his fields to tenants-at-will,* to raise his rents in order to pay the increased demand, or else, in cases where he has occupancy-tenants, he must either incur the expenses of a lawsuit in the rent court † or borrow money to pay the revenue demand. Anyhow he feels aggrieved at the apparently deliberate violation of the State's promises.

Unless, then, a settlement has been made with

* Owing to the density of population in parts of Oudh and North-Western Provinces, it is quite possible to exact a rack-rent from such tenants. The only check on the landowner is the force of custom or the fear that they will bolt. If he does not raise rents, he suffers from diminished income. Tenants-at-will, if ejected, have compensation for unexhausted improvements. In the North-Western-Provinces, it is only within the last four or five years that gradual enhancements have been authorised. In Bombay they have been demanded all at once.

† By an Act passed in 1873, settlement officers of the North-Western Provinces were empowered to fix the rents of occupancy-tenants at a rate equal to the Government demand. But this did not apply to districts where settlements had been already finished, of which there must be a large number, as settlement work had been going on regularly since 1860; nor does it apply to local cesses since imposed. Otherwise it is not possible to get rents raised, unless the landowner can show either that a field is being rented at a lower rate than similar fields held by the same class of tenants, or that he has, by wells or the like, added to the value of the soil. If a tenant does not pay rent he may be ejected by decree and lose his right. Occupancy rights are only heritable by those relatives who, at the decease of the last tenant, were working with him.

close regard to actual or fairly realisable assets, it is not surprising to find such general distress as was described by Sir William Muir, then Lieut.-Governor of the North-Western Provinces, in a memorandum * penned by him in March 1874: 'Whenever his camp passed through districts in which the land-tax had been materially increased, the Lieutenant-Governor was assailed by bitter complaints of loss and hardship among the people, and it cannot be otherwise. The landowners had during a whole generation enjoyed a certain income, and the expense of their families and retainers had long become adjusted thereto. Now when it was suddenly cut down, the outgoings could not be readily adjusted to the new income, and want and hardship must press somewhere. . . . The increase of the land revenue was followed

* I am indebted for this and other quotations to 'Our Land Revenue Policy in Northern India,' by C. J. Connell, Bengal Civil Service, 1876, Thacker, Spink, & Co. Anyone who wishes to go further into an intricate question will find ample information in that work. The rigidity of the revenue-system is especially criticised, and it is suggested that suitable suspensions of the land-tax, with 5 or 6 per cent. interest, should be authorised. This is obviously the simplest form of State loans. Mr. Justice Cunningham, one of the Famine Commissioners, before leaving India, published the draft of a Bill giving effect to this suggestion, which has, I believe, been also made by Mr. Buck, the head of the Agricultural Department of the North-Western Provinces. In a paper on the Bengal Famine of 1770, handed in by Sir G. Campbell to the Parliamentary Committee on Indian Public Works, I find that remissions of land-tax were frequently ordered by the Calcutta Government, and care was taken that they were also extended by the landlords to their tenants.

generally by a corresponding increase of rent, and the discontented cultivators added their cries to those of the landlords. The intensity of dissatisfaction and complaint, and the urgency of great bodies of petitioners pressing round the Lieutenant-Governor on these occasions, have been quite exceptional, only equalled, indeed, or surpassed by the declamation against the income-tax.' About the same time Mr. (now Sir) C. Bayley spoke to the same effect in Council. 'He believed that he was within the mark when he said that in the three-quarters of a century during which our Government had held the North-Western Provinces, there was scarcely a district in those provinces which had not suffered wholly or partially from over-assessment.'

It is superfluous to quote instances where the general results are admitted on such high authority. Although in parts of the North-Western Provinces the assessment is low, yet the burden has been so unequally distributed that there are districts, such as that of Cawnpore,* in which the peasant proprietors have been utterly crippled by the land-tax, and have been left to gnash their teeth in despair, as they see their ancestral estates gradually passing into the hands of strangers.

* See page 21, note *. According to an Article in *Calcutta Review*, vol. 53, 1873, out of 2,311 villages in the Cawnpore district, 69 per cent. had been up to that time transferred, besides a large number of portions of villages.

In Oudh the same over-assessment was found to have taken place, and the Chief Commissioner, with the strong approval of Lord Northbrook, ordered a revision to be made. In one district, Kheri, the landowners had saved themselves from debt by stoutly refusing to accept the revenue agreement, but others had had to sell their lands in the attempts to meet the State's demand. To take one instance out of many, in the Oudh Revenue Report of 1872, the officer in charge of the district of Hardui wrote as follows:—'As regards the collection of the land revenue, we shall soon have a new set of landlords. . . . The total of both sales and mortgages amounts to a third of the revenue of the district. It would be difficult to meet with a single village, except the larger talukas, in which the owners are free from debt, and the land free from incumbrance. I can affirm with confidence that the money, save a fraction or so borrowed during the year, was taken to pay revenue, and to no other purpose. The Zamindars have been, and are, unable to meet the enhanced assessment.' In spite of the revisions carried out by the local Government, it is to be feared that, owing to the rigidity with which the system of revenue administration is conducted, the present demand will be seen, at the expiration of the thirty years, to have pressed very heavily on the landowners, and to have forced them either into debt and sale of their lands, or into exaction of rack-rents from their unprotected tenants. The dense population of Oudh, and the large number of sub-proprietors, who absorb part of the rent, necessarily increase the pressure of what would otherwise be a light assessment.

In the Punjab, where the population is less dense, and large tracts of waste land have been reclaimed, and where great care was originally taken, for political reasons, to fix the assessment at a low rate, the pressure of the State demand has, it would appear, as yet proved less burdensome, although the increase of mortgages and transfers of land have recently been attracting attention even in that highly-favoured part of India, as well as in the Central Provinces.*

In Bombay,† where the difficulties of the settle-

* Deccan Ryots' Report, pages 161–173 of Appendix A. The Chief Commissioner, Colonel Keatinge, writes, 'The liability of land for sale for debt is the natural and logical corollary of the conferment of the proprietary right. But he cannot conceal from himself that the boon cannot be conceded in those parts of India with which he is acquainted without serious political danger. The owners of the land, as a rule, still possess great influence, whilst they are undoubtedly, as a class, ignorant of affairs and hereditarily extravagant. The city men, who purchase large estates, are, on the other hand, mere money-lenders and usurers, and disliked by the country people, and possessing no political influence whatever.' In the Report for 1878-9, the Commissioner of one district writes, 'Thus the proprietary rights in 339 estates were either sold or mortgaged during the year. The cause, as I believe, lies in our legal system.'

† I have not referred to the land-revenue system of Madras, for the simple reason that Sir G. Campbell, in his chapter on 'Tenure of Land in India,' in the Cobden Club series, says

ment officer are increased by the fact that he has no rent as a guide, there is good reason for supposing that one of the causes which intensified the distress among the Deccan ryots was the too heavy assessments of poor soils, and the sudden enhancement of the State's demands, whereby the peasantry, already pressed hard by their creditors, and embarrassed by the sudden fall of prices, found their resources still further curtailed. In fact, the Bombay Government admitted that this was the case in certain districts where it

that 'The official documents are such that he, an expert of many provinces, shrinks from them. An ordinary Englishman might as well attempt to read an arrow-headed inscription.' But a Report of the Madras Board of Revenue made in 1869, quoted by him, informs us that 'The bulk of the people are paupers. They can just pay their cess in a good year, and fail altogether in a bad. Remissions have to be made perhaps in every third year in most districts. There is a bad year in some one district or group of districts every year.' The famine of 1877 is a striking commentary on this. In Bombay and Madras the salt-tax within the last ten years has been raised from 1 rupee 8 annas per maund (80 lbs.) to 2 rupees 8 annas. Bombay has to pay a local cess of £217,500, Madras of £546,000, imposed in 1869 and 1871.—*Gazette of India*, March 15, 1879. The Madras Settlement operations which have been going on of late have, I believe, resulted in an increase of the land revenue. I do not know whether sudden enhancements have been sanctioned by the Madras authority. In some Bombay districts the original enhancements reached as high as 225 per cent., and a rise from 80 to 100 per cent. was quite common. Moreover, it appears to have been the idea of some settlement officers that poor soils could yield as much rent as rich ones—the result being that the wretched cultivator had hardly anything left to live on. This was going on in the teeth of Sir George Wingate's theory of assessment thirty years ago.

ordered a reduction to be made. In a petition presented to the collector of Sholapur by the ryots of Karmala Taluka, September 1875, it is stated: 'Since 1818 the inhabitants of the native States, such as Hyderabad, Indore, Gwalior, Baroda, Nagpore, &c., owing to oppression, used to migrate into the British dominions. Of late, in consequence of the heavy assessment and injustice caused by oppressive laws, there has been a discordance between the ryots, sowkars, and Government, the result of which is that many ryots, sowkars, &c., have given up their lands, estates, &c., and have been migrating to the native States.' This is not a pleasing result of our enlightened rule.

But it must not be supposed that when a settlement has been made for thirty years that the Government will not, like Oliver Twist, 'ask for more.' By an ingenious fiction, of which, as of others equally ingenious, Sir J. Strachey is generally looked upon as the distinguished author, local cesses, now amounting in the North-Western Provinces to 18 P.C. on half the rental, have been imposed on the land-owning classes on the theory that they pay such cesses as distinct from land-revenue, *quâ* citizens not *quâ* landowners. Thus, under Lord Mayo's Decentralisation Scheme* of 1869, the North-Western Provinces and Oudh have to pay a fresh contribution of £426,000, the Punjab of £190,000, Bom-

* See Appendix III.

bay of £217,500, the Central Provinces of £24,000; while, under the so-called Famine Insurance Scheme of 1877, the North-Western Provinces and Oudh pay £110,000, Punjab £49,000, and the Central Provinces £12,000.* And this additional tax on the agricultural classes has been imposed after they had good reason for believing that they would not be liable to any further demand in this shape till a new thirty years' settlement. It is this—to their minds—flagrant breach of faith, more perhaps than the actual amount of taxation, that is to be especially remembered.

But assuming that in spite of local cesses the State's demand still remains moderate, and

* I have not mentioned the two Bengal cesses of 1871 and 1877, £678,000, the Madras 1871 cess £546,000; nor have I included the patwari (revenue officials) funds, £230,000, in the North-Western Provinces, and £245,000 in Madras, because, according to the *Gazette of India*, March 15, 1879, 'There are similar officials throughout India, but the payments made to them, and the revenue intercepted for the purpose, are for the most part excluded from the accounts. The patwari fund of the North-Western Provinces and Madras do not therefore imply additional taxation.' But it must be remembered, as has been pointed out to me, that a fixed rate on rentals comes heavier than the previously existing loose kind of payments, partly in grain and grants of land, partly in money. The native, no doubt, regards the fund as fresh taxation. It is one more turn of the screw. In Oudh, at present, the revenue officials and village watchmen receive hardly anything direct from Government; but if a fund were to be formed by the imposition of about 10 per cent. on the rental, as has been done in the North-Western Provinces, this would be to all intents and purposes additional taxation, although it might be called 'change in the form of accounts.'

no sudden enhancement has prevented the landowner from readjusting himself to it, yet a year of scarcity with a rigid system of exacting the land-revenue may work great havoc among the agricultural classes. The Government orders the landowners to pay up; and the latter, being for the most part poor men, in turn are obliged to exact the whole of their rents, whatever has been the out-turn of the crops. The hired labourers* who are employed by land-

* The hired labourer is always on the verge of starvation. He earns *2d.* to *3d.* a day when work can be got. In parts of Oudh he makes up 20 per cent. of the population. After a season of scarcity he soon collapses. I have heard of well-disposed landowners supporting him in bad times. They might perhaps do more in this direction if revenue were suspended. In the best of times high prices tell heavily against the man who neither owns nor rents any land. He is very often the predial serf—though unrecognised by English law—of the grain-dealer or landowner, who promises to keep him and his family alive in return for their services. I have heard wonderful stories, illustrating the honour of the lowest classes, of such serfs working off their debts—invalid by law—by taking service with Englishmen. Out of 190 millions in British India, labourers, chiefly agricultural, are estimated at 30 millions, or 16 per cent. Last year, after the heavy rainfall, there was frightful mortality from fever, especially among the poorest class in the North-Western Provinces and Oudh; according to the recent sanitary report, an increase of over 900,000 on the average rate. How far this was the result of the debility caused by the famine of 1877-8 it is difficult to say; but there would appear to be a good deal of truth in the opinion of one officer, who reported 'That the disease is aggravated by want of food, which at all times prevails amongst the lowest classes.'—*Pioneer*, February 7, 1880. An article of the same paper, February 11, 1880, on 'Sanitation,' says, 'It is obvious that the improved registration of deaths is disclosing to the Government a condition of affairs among the people, and a liability to

owners on their home-farms, or by high-caste tenants, soon die off like rotten sheep. The tenants-at-will disappear next, their savings invested in ornaments and stores of grain being soon spent in paying up rent and then buying grain at high prices; the better class of tenants get into debt, while the landowners, after screwing out what rent they can, find themselves obliged to mortgage their lands. The Government opens relief works, and by lavish expenditure manages to save the lives of those—chiefly the lowest classes—who are willing and able to come to them. But if this gigantic system of poor relief is combined with strict exaction of the land-tax, the better classes have nothing but ruin to stare them in the face. If the famine is prolonged, they may, so far from being able to help others, have themselves to seek relief or to starve. Even when suspensions of revenue are authorised, the relief is very inadequate, and often

suffer from high prices, of which there was formerly but little knowledge.' I may as well here state for the benefit of English readers that the *Pioneer* is the most official in tone of the papers of Northern India. Its admissions are therefore all the more valuable. Two members of the Indian Famine Commission, Mr. Caird and Mr. Sullivan, write, 'Already the wages of the landless class bear a less proportion to the price of food than in any country of which we have knowledge.' The export trade of grain goes on during famine, for the simple reason that it does not pay traders to sell it in India. The above-mentioned members of the Commission suggest that the State should store grain in inaccessible parts of India; but would it not be better not to deplete the people's own stores? The natives of India have learnt that the best way of providing against famine is to keep food.

granted too late, and the arrears are got in before the land has had time to recover.

'The structure of Indian society is, in some ways,' write the Famine Commissioners, 'admirably adapted for common effort against a common misfortune. The ordinary form of life in the Hindoo family makes each individual a member of a corporate body, in whose possessions, rights, and duties he participates, and to which he is legally entitled to look for assistance in time of need. Even where the legal right does not exist, the moral obligation of mutual association is scarcely less distinctly recognised. Apart from family ties, there are other relationships, such as those of landlord and tenant, master and servant, employer of agricultural labour and employed, alms-giver and alms-receiver, which are of the utmost importance in binding the social fabric together and enabling it to resist any ordinary strain. There are, too, salutary habits of frugality and foresight, the precious result of traditional experience, which have an all-important bearing upon the power of Indian society to pass comparatively unscathed through periods of dearth. Any form of relief calculated to bring these rights into obscurity or desuetude, or to break down these habits by showing them to be superfluous, would be an incalculable misfortune.'

It is this undesirable consequence that seems to be directly brought about by the Indian Government. Mr. C. A. Elliott's Report on the Mysore

Famine is invaluable in showing what is the logical outcome of the present inelastic system of collecting the land-tax. He says (page 8): 'I consider the Mysore ryot to be, or to have been, better off than any class of cultivators in any province of India that I am acquainted with. The land-tax does not exceed one-tenth or one-eighth of the value of the gross produce at ordinary prices. The demand fixed in Pirnia's time (under native rule) has been unaltered till now, except where the Settlement Department has introduced its new assessment, and that department has wisely abstained from exacting any considerable increase.' But in spite of this advantage, 'the ownership of the land is fast passing out of the hands of those directly interested in it.' The country had, according to Administration Reports quoted by Mr. Elliott, suffered in former years from deficient rainfall, but actual famine* had been staved off by the consumption 'of the surplus ragi stored in underground pits, from which it is withdrawn in times of scarcity, as the grain will keep sound and good for forty or fifty years.'

The first warning of the last famine was given in October 1875, by the Deputy Commissioner of Chitaldrug, who proposed remission of revenue and free right of grazing on unoccupied lands. This was granted in a few districts; but it is to be noticed that, though the ryots petitioned elsewhere for

* See Appendix IV.

remission of revenue, and though, after allowing for consumption, there was, according to the Report (page 191), no surplus out of which to pay revenue, yet more money was squeezed out of the ryot during 1875–6 than in the previous year of plenty. 'To do this they must have opened their grain-pits and parted, to some extent, with their bullion.' Next year the ryot did not produce enough by 340,000 tons to feed himself, but he had to pay 75 lakhs (i.e. £750,000) in taxes, two-thirds of the usual amount, 'and must have done this by selling ornaments and parting with hoarded bullion.' In December 1877, 'the revenue officers were exerting themselves to realise the Government demand for the year, as well as arrears of past years. This was a matter which required delicate handling, for it was easy to conceive that the exaction of the demand now might force the ryot at a subsequent time to become an applicant for Government aid. It appeared on inquiry that a great number of ryots had had their rights sold up for arrears, and this as a mere matter of routine.'

Well might the *Pioneer*, when reviewing Mr. Elliott's Report, ask, 'Is it possible for short-sightedness to go further than this? Before the famine actually sets in, the revenue is rigidly exacted, so that stores of grain and bullion are exhausted, and when at its height the Government is spending thousands of pounds, we find the ryot being sold up and coming on the relief works. It is only in 1877-8, when the famine is declining, that adequate relief is given by postponement of revenue. . . . . But, though the authorities at last began to learn wisdom, yet it came too late. The famine expenditure cost the State 110 lakhs of rupees, that is to say, more than one year's revenue, but the cost to the people has been infinitely greater. The province has lost 9¾ millions sterling in produce, a quarter of a million in cattle, and more than a million human lives.' Such is one outrageous instance of red-tapism, which strains at a gnat and swallows a camel.

But Mysore is not the only part of India that has been treated in this way. In 1877 the North-West Provinces and Oudh were visited with drought, and there was great deficiency in the yield of the autumn crop, on which the poor part of the population depend for food.

* The Local Government proposed suspension of revenue demand; but was reminded (*vide* Annual Report for 1877-8) that, 'With reference to the character of the settlement, proposals or promises for remission ought not to be encouraged,' and that 'it would be a direct encouragement of unthrift if the demand were even to be suspended on any great scale.' The confident expectation was expressed that 'the great bulk of the autumn instalments would be collected at the ordinary

* See Appendix XII.

season, and suspension would be granted only in cases where they were absolutely necessary.'

Commenting on this, the *Pioneer*, in an article of August 26, 1879, said: 'It must be recollected that the autumn crops had then been nearly everywhere lost, and it was notorious that the Jhansi district had been ruined by inopportune revenue collections not ten years before. What were the consequences? The district officers were compelled to yield obedience, and those who can read between the lines of the Annual Report, where it is mildly remarked that "Perhaps less indulgence was shown in some instances than circumstances might have justified," will have no difficulty in realising the effect on village communities of these harsh instructions. The statements of the registration officer show that "some thirty thousand registered sales of the value of 37 lakhs were the direct result of the failure of the *Kharif* of the year under report."'

In a letter addressed to *The Times* some months ago, Mr. C. A. Elliott, who pointed out the result of revenue collections in Mysore, made an attempt to hide from the public what took place in the North-West Provinces and Oudh in 1877-8, but the Local Authorities of those provinces tell their own tale in unmistakable language:—'That much of the money paid into the State treasury by the landlords was borrowed from money-lenders, the great increase in the numbers of documents registered would tend to show.'—(*Administration Report of* 1877–78). If the drought had been continued, there would have been, as far as can be seen, an exact repetition of the Mysore catastrophe. The financial authorities at Calcutta forced the local government against its will to collect revenue, and the result is what was to be expected. Some years hence we shall probably hear of a Bill for the relief of the distressed landowners of these Provinces who have been bound to the Procrustean couch of bureaucratic routine.

But even when the horrors of hunger are over and the fields are again golden with ripening grain, the hand of the State lies hard upon them. Under a deep, 'a religious sense of the obligation,' that it must do something to ward off famine, a compassionate Government imposes, as has been already mentioned, a further tax upon agriculture, and then* appropriates the money for general purposes, perhaps to pay for a war, perhaps to make some fiscal reform, involving a loss of £250,000, which has in turn to be recovered by vexatious direct taxation.

Meanwhile the land is further drained, and exposed to famine.

Such is the rigorous and vigorous land-revenue

* According to the last financial statement, the proceeds of the famine taxes for three years amount to £3,393,891. The expenditure on famine relief is £417,420. What has been done with the rest? Sir J. Strachey says, 'It has quite fulfilled its object.' No doubt the tax-payer has developed a 'sense of obligation.' Was this the object? See Appendix III.

system (utterly unlike 'the rough annual bargain' which took place under Hindoo and Mahomedan rule) that has been imposed on India, in the belief that what works well in England must necessarily work well in India. Is not thrift good? and is not thrift encouraged by being able to calculate on the future? and is not this secured by fixing the land revenue for a given period, and collecting it whether there is a crop or not? Alas! few Anglo-Indian officials will now deny there is a sad fallacy underlying all this plausible argument, and the only certain outlook is ruin and death. As Carlyle says, we may make our bank notes and circulate them, but if there is nothing to correspond to them, Nature refuses to cash them, and the poor creature who has to present them to her starves.

The variable amount of rainfall in India invalidates this rigid way of looking at things. It is an awkward fact, but men cannot live without food, and the grain which goes to pay rent and revenue demands, cannot at the same time be retained to support the producer.

But then, does not the cultivator, with all the apparatus of roads and railways, make a fine profit in years of plenty? Well, perhaps he does secure enough to go a pilgrimage by rail or on foot, or to trick out his wife and children with some bangles, and they prove useful supplies to fall back on; but very often—for beasts will die, especially if short of fodder—he has to buy a new bullock, and sometimes—for he has a hard life of it on the whole--he indulges in a grand piece of extravagant feasting at a daughter's marriage. Or perhaps he thinks it a duty—strangely primitive mortal that he is—to pay off ancestral debt, and then—so consistent is he—he signs a heavy bond without thinking of the interest charged, and leaves a legacy of debt for his children and grandchildren.

Moreover, his fatalistic creed, the result partly of his natural environment, partly of traditional ideas, does not allow him to look very far into the future, and, feeling the evil or good of each day sufficient, he makes merry while he may.

Hence a system which presupposes physical conditions and moral powers other than actually exist, or are likely to exist, in India, must obviously prove disastrous. High* officials are beginning to openly admit this truth, of which many a district officer, and even the high official, when he lived among the people, has been for a long time past convinced, and perhaps under the influence of an enlightened public opinion in England some regard will be paid to the teaching of sad experience.

But the bureaucratic mind does not easily con-

* The debate on the Deccan Ryots Relief Bill was very interesting, for the revelations of opinions which it elicited from high quarters. After the orders sent down to the Government of the North-Western Provinces and Oudh in 1877-8, it was curious to hear Sir J. Strachey reprobating the severity of the present revenue system. 'It is not that the assessment is too heavy, but that the procedure under which it is levied is too rigid.'

sent to burn the idols which it has so long worshipped. A few years ago, Mr. Hunter attracted some attention to the question of Indian famines by publishing a pamphlet on the relation between droughts and sunspots. The prediction of years of scarcity may ultimately prove useful in suggesting methods of meeting their periodical recurrence, but hitherto the Indian Government seems to have greedily seized at the idea as justifying the imposition of fresh taxation.

It would, indeed, be a very convenient method of getting rid of responsibilities, if famines and all their consequences could be wholly ascribed to the action of the sun. When the cause is millions of miles away, what can the most benevolent Government do, except first show its sense of obligation to prevent its effects by levying famine insurance taxes, and then its sense of reliance on Providence by appropriating for general purposes the moneys so raised? But ordinary men will perhaps think it as well not to lose sight of any conditions which are within human control.

> The remedies oft in ourselves do lie
> Which we ascribe to heaven, the fated sky
> Gives us free scope, only doth backward pull
> Our slow designs, when we ourselves are dull.

It is obvious from the above description of the land revenue system, that the pressure of taxation under this head may vary indefinitely, not only in different districts according to the greater or less density of population, but also within short periods in the same district, owing to the variation of rainfall. In short, the land revenue, if rigidly collected, may represent anything, from a share of a fair rent corresponding to the margin of profit between the best and worst soils, in years of plenty, to a grinding and desolating tax on subsistence in years of scarcity. And even in good years a half share of rents, if the latter have been unnaturally forced up by the necessity of meeting an excessive State demand, may be a heavy tax on the agricultural classes, while more than a half share—as is often the case—of fair rents, still more of rack rents, will prove proportionately heavier.

Moreover, although at the beginning of a 30 years' settlement the State's demand may not prove too heavy for any particular district, yet if the population has greatly increased, and the produce of the land does not increase proportionately, the same assessment may be an overwhelming burden at the end of the settlement.

In recent controversies in England about the incidence of taxation in India, it has been too often forgotten that, if different periods are compared, the same land revenue when less per head, and so seemingly lighter, may yet really be heavier, unless the persons, among whom it is divided, are adding their share to the general wealth.

But one of the results of British rule is the increase of the non-productive agricultural population, while the wealth that might support them goes out of the country.

What the Chief Commissioner of Oudh wrote about that province in 1873 is true, though to a less extent, of the rest of India. 'It is owing to our system that the * thousands who formerly aided the soil with their earnings sent from afar are now living on it a dead burden, where they were formerly an active support. It is owing to our system that girls are reared in hundreds, not only to be so many more mouths to feed, but to involve their fathers in still deeper debt, to meet their marriage expenses. It is owing to our system that men are no longer allowed to kill each other by scores in agrarian quarrels, that the march of famine and epidemic disease (?) is checked. . . . Owing to the operation of these causes the population which has only to look to the land for their support is annually becoming more and

* In Oudh, owing to the disbanding of native armies and retainers, there has been a large addition made to the rural population. The abolition of native courts and armies must have had a similar effect all over India. When it is remembered that a native family of five can live comfortably on about £5 to £6 a year, it is obvious that the wealth, between four and five million pounds, which goes out of the country annually to pay for non-productive expenditure, must make a serious difference in so poor a country. If one goes to a well-governed native state like Jeypore, one sees how large a part of the revenues is diffused again among the people.

more numerous. The consequences are not difficult to foresee. When the land cannot yield more than is sufficient for the mouths dependent on its produce, it follows that there is nothing left wherewith to meet the demands of the State or any other demand.'

But even in those parts of India where there is still much waste land to be reclaimed, it must be remembered that the loss of fodder caused by such reclamation increases the mortality of cattle, and the cultivated land is impoverished not only by the loss of the droppings of the cattle which die, but also by the use of dung-cakes as fuel. The present prosperity and future improvement of Indian agriculture pivots on the bullock. It has been found impossible to get the peasant to use a more efficient plough, even if he could afford to buy it, because the ordinary bullock is not strong enough to draw it. The Agricultural Department of the North-West Provinces has had various models prepared, but it would appear that in mute protest at their weight 'procumbit humi bos.'

In an interesting, though somewhat egotistical pamphlet on 'Agricultural Reform in India,'* Mr. A. Hume goes so far as to write as follows: 'Owing to a variety of causes, agriculture in India

* Mr. Hume was Secretary to the Revenue, Agriculture, and Commerce Department of the Indian Government, until it was amalgamated last year with the Home Department, at a saving of about £9,000 per annum.

has become, and becomes daily, more and more what Liebig has happily designated a system of spoliation. . . . It is clear that a time must arrive when by continually taking a great deal and putting back very little, both purse and soil are exhausted. . . . Yet from another and distinct source ruin and desolation, more palpable and speedy in its course, though more limited in its operation, await vast tracts in Northern India, unless the voice of reason can gain a hearing, and science be allowed to guide agriculture. In Oudh, the Punjab, and the North-West Provinces, the soils contain an appreciable admixture of saline particles. With the construction of high level canals the subsoil water level is raised, the surface flooded, the earth yields up its soluble salts to the water, which again restores them (but on the surface) as it passes away in vapour. At first the result may be good. . . . Time passes on, some crops begin to be unprofitable; in the hottest time of year a glimmer, as though of hoar frost, overspreads the land. The land grows worse and worse, but ever night and day nature works slowly on, and the time comes when, abandoned by the cultivator, the land glitters white and waste, as though thickly strewn with crisp, new-fallen snow; never, alas! to melt away, except under the rays of science. Along the little old Western Jumna Canal thousands of fields are to be seen thus sterilised. Along the course of the mighty Ganges—a work, as it were, but of yesterday—the dreary wintry-looking rime is already in many places creeping over the soil . . . The time must come when some of the richest arable tracts of Northern India will have become howling saline deserts.'

There may be good reason for thinking that Mr. Hume, in his desire to carry certain reforms, has overstated his case as regards the gradual deterioration of land all over India.* Many men

* The spread of *reh*, or saline efflorescence over parts of Northern India is an undeniable fact. As canals are supposed to have a good deal to do with it, they are at present in rather bad odour, in spite of their good service in the recent famines. Efforts are being made to increase, where it is possible, the number of wells, a system of irrigation familiar to the native. Moreover, as they entail greater toil in raising the water, he is prevented from drenching the land. The difficulty of the various taxes for canal water is avoided. Sir A. Cotton's proposal to spend thirty millions sterling on canals is of a very questionable value, as far as Northern India is concerned. It is asserted by district officers that in some places the water supply of wells is drained away by the canals, while in others, after a heavy rainfall, the land gets waterlogged by the stoppage of the drainage. The great success of the Madras irrigation system appears to be due to the heavy rainfall on the Western Ghauts, and the much greater declivity which is to be found there than in the great plain of Northern India. Nor is the soil saline. See Appendix IV.

In a recent lecture at the Society of Arts, Mr. Robertson, author of the 'Report of the Tour in Coimbatore,' speaking of Madras, says, 'Experienced men positively assert that the deterioration during the last thirty years has been not less than 30 per cent. Under the rent settlement now in force, a premium is offered for bad farming.' He complains of want of manure and desiccation. Although the native puts the ashes of his manure-fuel on the land, and thereby returns its chemical elements, yet the straw part, so useful for retaining moisture, is lost. Mr. Hume calculates the average annual loss of cattle at ten million beasts, who have had large experience in matters connected with the land and who have done their best to find out the truth on this very difficult question, would, no doubt, regard the above statement as very exaggerated, though they would admit—as everyone admits—that the loss of fuel and fodder as the area of cultivation increases, is a very serious set-off against the improvement of agriculture caused by pressure of population, and undoubtedly tends to impoverish the soil. It is obvious that where such an enormous area as one million square miles is concerned, there is ample room for difference of conditions and consequently of opinions, and an outsider can merely record the fact that grave fears as to the future of Indian agriculture are entertained by men like Mr. Hume and Mr. Robertson, who profess to have carefully investigated the subject.

But whether the soil of India is deteriorating or not, there can be no doubt that under British rule the population, except so far as it is thinned periodically by famine, is overtaking the means of

and asserts that one half of the whole capitalised wealth of ninety-nine hundredths of the whole population of India is in their cattle. He estimates roughly one hundred millions of cattle (£75,000,000) for the whole of India.

The native landowner does not seem to have much encouragement in making wells, as the State, though contributing nothing except perhaps a loan, for which it receives interest, gets a half share of the profits at a new settlement. Perhaps, if it were generally understood that an actual reduction of the State demand should be made in consideration of each well, he might be more willing to invest money this way. The State would incur less famine outlay.

subsistence. The terrible mortality during the recent famines followed by the rapid recovery in the land revenue proves—unless great cruelty has been shown in its collection—that there was a few years ago a large non-productive population. Manufactures and mines may in the future absorb some of it, but at present free trade has only increased the difficulties of the situation. Lancashire competition has, admittedly, taken the bread out of the mouths of native weavers, and has thrown them back on the land for a livelihood. In a year of scarcity these extra mouths have to be filled at the cost of the State.

If the millions spent on famine relief, partly in consequence of the extra rural population caused by foreign competition, be set off against the gains in cheaper cotton goods, it may be doubted whether the economical results are such as they are reckoned to be. A number of paupers periodically fed by outdoor relief—for this is what it practically comes to —is in part the outcome of *unlimited* free trade *suddenly* introduced, without regard to the special conditions of Indian agriculture and the iron bonds of the Indian caste system. The usual arguments, unanswerable as they are, when applied to countries with an active-minded population, are not equally conclusive, when applied to a country where movement is very slow.*

* After writing the above, I was glad to find such a great authority as the late W. Bagehot insisting, in his *Economic*

In England free trade was introduced *ab intra* under the pressure of a gradually enlightened public opinion; in India it has been forced *ab extra* on a for-the-most-part ignorant and unlettered population. Hence the intelligence, which in the former case brought about the change, was able to readjust itself to new conditions, but in the latter case the intelligence was that of the rulers only, while the ruled still retain their deeply-rooted prejudices. The custom-bound native of India, not knowing where to turn for daily bread, opposed to emigration—the great safety valve of over-populated European countries—and reluctant even to migrate* to any distance, betakes himself to the already over-burdened land, the surplus† produce of which

Studies, on the absurdity of the claim of Political Economy to be an universal science, irrespective of the conditions of society. (See Appendix VI.)

* The Chief Commissioner of the Central Provinces recently tried to colonise some of the waste parts of the Central Provinces, but the scheme proved impracticable. The native of India has none of the colonist's enterprise, and merely works outwards from the village centre. He is devoted to his village home.

† The total annual drain of capital from India is now over £16,000,000. Of this two and a-half millions is interest on debt; four and three-quarter millions guaranteed interest; three and three-quarter millions is for superannuation, furlough, &c. allowances, nearly one million for army charges, and two millions for stores of all sorts. Of course, a part of this wealth may be said, though there is no proof, to be the creation of our Government, and a great part is payment for so-called reproductive expenditure. But still it is a very heavy drain on a country where £5 a-year can almost keep a family. Taxation helps to make the railways pay, by forcing trade in grain. Then taxes are imposed, because trade is flourishing!! (See Appendix VII.)

has to be exported to pay for interest on debt, pensions, troops, transports, and the like.

During the ten years 1869–1878, the expenditure in England reached the enormous sum of £104,704,064, being one-fifth of the total expenditure of the Indian Government during that decade. Is it possible for a country with such a teeming population to stand this drain? If only half of it had been spent in India, it would have supported nearly one million families—the number calculated to have died in the recent famine. In spite of these figures Mr. Bright speaks of India as a burden on England. The truth is that scientific bloodsucking has taken the place of promiscuous plunder, but the result for India is equally bad; she is gradually losing her capital, while her population increases, and periodical famines stare her in the face.

Railways are no direct remedy against famine; they bring food, but it is at very high prices, and the State has to pay for it by taxation. On the other hand, each fresh line increases the steady drain in the shape of interest, for it is well known that only one-tenth of the whole debt of India is held by natives, although the loans are taken up by brokers in India. Among the 60,000 shareholders of the capital raised for railways there are only 317 natives, while about one-half of the capital has been spent in England. The old custom of allowing small sums of money to flow into the various treasuries has of late years been abandoned, and offers of great banking firms are preferred. It is not so much taxation *per se* that is oppressive, but the non-return of taxation to the people in the shape of wages.

In fact, the Government of India, as Mr. Hyndman has pointed out, is becoming more and more like a great absentee landlord; and the natural consequence may be seen in the history of Ireland, Turkey, and Egypt. To develop the resources of a young country like Australia or New Zealand by means of foreign capital is one thing. to attempt the same with an old country like India is quite another. That which helps to populate the former only tends to depopulate the latter. India's borrowings ought to be limited by the supplies which she can draw from her own children.

The theory of redeeming a vast continent with a dense population and an ancient civilisation by the mechanism of money is an outrageous fallacy, which could be only entertained by a nation whose insight into the true dynamics of human life and action has been obscured by its intense worship of wealth.

What Burke said a century ago, in the debate on Fox's India Bill, when comparing the effects of the irruptions of Arabs, Tartars, and Persians with those of British conquest, has still some truth in it:—'Poverty, sterility, and desolation are not a recreating prospect to the eye of man; and there are very few that can bear to grow old among the curses of a whole people. If their passion or their avarice drove the Tartar lords to acts of rapacity or tyranny, there was time enough even in the short life of man, to bring round the ill effects of the abuse of power upon the power itself. If hoards were made by violence, they were still domestic hoards, and domestic profusion or the rapine of a more powerful and prodigal hand, restored them to the people. With the many disorders and few political checks on power, nature had still fair play; the sources of acquisition were not dried up, and therefore the trade, the manufactures, and the commerce of the country flourished. . . . . But under the English Government all this order is reversed; but it is our protection that destroys India. It was their enmity, but it is our friendship.'

Englishmen ought never to lose sight of this running sore, which must be healed as far as possible if India is to support its ever expanding population. As it is the order maintained by British Government that has enabled the vast population of India to exist, it is its duty as well as its interest to take every possible step to maintain it. It has pledged itself—whether wisely or unwisely—if not absolutely to prevent, yet at least to mitigate the horrors of famine; it is bound, therefore, not to allow an inelastic revenue system to cripple its peasantry, or the clamours of Lancashire to burden the land

* *E.g.*—The payment of £50,000 for the Madras Irrigation Company's bankrupt business; the unnecessary flinging away of three millions sterling in the purchase of the East Indian Railway.

with taxation, or the greed of interested speculators and the glory* of ambitious soldiers to prevent the accumulation of those resources which it has undertaken to husband.

* It is well known that the Horse-Guards has for years past opposed army reform in India, for fear of losing patronage. More than one Indian Finance Minister has protested against the home military charges unfairly put on India. The best way for England to contribute towards the Afghan War would be to re-adjust these charges. Sir T. Seccombe, in his evidence before the Public Works Committee, alluded to the injustice of the present arrangement,

CHAPTER III.

THE next most important feature of British rule is the administration of justice. Its far-reaching consequences are often forgotten by men whose experience is confined to England. But in a country like India, where, owing to the enormous number of non-wage-receiving persons engaged in agriculture, there are endless sources of small disputes arising out of petty debts incurred to meet some sudden call, or in the case of coparcenary bodies out of partition of profits or shares in the soil, the procedure of the courts has a most intimate bearing on the lives of the masses.

On this head it may be safely asserted that there is a growing opinion among officers, well acquainted with the working of our courts, that they have become 'an hissing and a reproach.'

Thus, Mr. Hume writes, 'we have wasted on an elaborate, cumbrous, and unsuitable system of civil jurisprudence, money that ought to have been employed in improving our agriculture and increasing the material comforts of the masses. . . . . The system on which it was expended has been the chief and direct cause of the major portion of the indebtedness and impoverishment of our agriculturists. Errors as to tenures; forcing proprietary rights upon people incapable of appreciating or understanding them; forcing upon districts where one system of landholding was indigenous a wholly different, exotic, and therefore unsuitable one; the want of elasticity in our system of realising the revenue, unlimited subdivision of holdings, and a dozen other causes, may be indicated as having, our *courts being as they are*, contributed to it, but these courts themselves are the *fons et origo* of the evil, and had they been the simple summary courts of equity and not of law, which was all the state of the country demanded, all these other causes would have smouldered on almost innoxiously.'

Mr. Hume then goes on to describe the enormous revolution which has been the result of English law courts. While under native rule no private person had, broadly speaking, any property in the soil, but only a high class of occupancy right, heritable but not transferable, all proprietary right being vested directly in the state or vicariously in some powerful chief or official, we have conferred rights on landowners and under-proprietors, thereby largely increasing their facilities for incurring debts, which they have often been too eager to use to their own destruction. While under native rule the money-lender lent only to a few, and from fear of violence seldom realised his nominally usurious rates of interest, and received a kind of annuity from the community in which he lived, we have, by the grant of transferable rights in land and by rigid collection of revenue, encouraged the professional money-lender, and by the* costliness and technicalities of our law courts have sharpened his claws, while we have cut those of his victim, by depriving him of the use of his club.

'Thus, with our innovations we have dissolved the bonds of society, we have turned peace into war, we have arrayed every class against that on which it was most dependent, capitalists against

* Appendix B. of the Deccan Ryots Commission's Report, is full of information on the action of the Law and Civil Courts on the agricultural debtor. The difficulty of getting the native into court, owing to the cost of employing a pleader and summoning witnesses, the distance of courts—in some parts of India—from his home, and the waste of time, are the chief complaints. Then, there may be an appeal, with all its further costs. The procedure is the same for a debt of 5 rupees as for 5,000. The shrewd and well-to-do moneylender has evidently the best of it as against the stupid and poor peasant. The ignorance and thoughtlessness of the latter is illustrated in every page of the above report. 'The aid given by law to moneylenders and borrowers is all on the side of the former; the latter have no protection whatever. They should have all; the former require none, being well able to take care of themselves. I believe that nine-tenths of the disturbances in India are attributable to this source.' According to inquiries made by Mr. Hope, as regard the relations of moneylenders and peasantry in a number of native States such as Hydrabad, Baroda, &c., it appears that in all these States civil suits for debt are comparatively rare. Summary inquiry into the facts of the case, with scrutiny of accounts, and more or less rough and ready adaptation of the creditor's demands to the debtor's means is the common practice. Usurer's business is kept within bounds, but not stopped. See speech at introduction of Deccan Ryots Relief Bill in *Gazette of India.* For the nature of this Bill, see Appendix VIII.

landowners, landlords against tenants, every man almost against his fellow.'

Nor does Mr. Hume stand alone in his denunciation of our civil procedure. In the debate on the Deccan Ryots Relief Bill, Mr. Hope, C.S.I., who represented the Bombay Government in the Legislative Council, used language quite as strong. 'Looking,' he said, 'to the fact that out of about 1,400,000 civil suits of all kinds disposed of annually by the courts of all grades in British India, some 1,200,000 or 85 per cent. are for sums under 100 rupees (£8), and 630,000 or 44 per cent. for sums less than 20 rupees, I cannot but feel, and I think the people feel too, that our Civil Procedure Code, with its 650 sections and all that they involve, is in a majority of cases a burden almost too heavy to be borne. I trust that the day will come when not only the Deccan ryots, but all India, will obtain relief in this respect.' Mr. Hope only repeats the convictions of many others who have watched the working of British courts and codes. Thus, in 1862 the Governor of Bombay writes: 'His lordship in council entertains no doubt of the fact that the labouring classes of the native community suffer enormous injustice from the want of protection by law from the extortionate practices of moneylenders. He believes that our civil courts have become hateful to the masses of our Indian subjects, from being made the instruments of the almost incredible rapacity of usurious capitalists. Nothing can be more calculated to give rise to widespread discontent and disaffection to the British Government than the practical working of the present law.'

The Blue-books on the Deccan riots yield abundance of evidence as to what is the feeling of the natives on the matter. The Collector of Ahmednagar writes in 1874 as follows, with reference to some villagers formerly under the Nizam's Government, but then enjoying the blessings of the English courts:—'One and all assured me that they wanted to have nothing to do with our civil courts, they have suffered no loss from want of them, but that now they have been established they will soon suffer much, and their lands be taken from them and given to the sowkars (money-lenders). . . . I may add that the little I have seen of the prosperous state of a few Mogalai villages adjoining our own, but not cursed with our civil law system, fully confirms the truth of what these people urged.' Here is a crucial experiment made by the natives themselves, and their view is expressed with a simple truthfulness, which ought to penetrate the bosom of the most ardent worshipper of the Civil Procedure Code.

No one can doubt that this sentiment of the Bombay ryot would be re-echoed throughout India, if opportunity were given for its expression, and that there would be a grand bonfire of civil codes in every village, if British force were withdrawn.

The increasing number of transfers of landed property through the action of the civil courts was the cause of a lengthy official discussion in India during the years 1873-4.

There seems to have been general agreement, first, that the compulsory sale of hereditary land was very distasteful to the people, and might again be the cause of grave political danger,* as it proved in the Mutiny of 1857; secondly, that transfer of property was going on at an undesirable rate.

This was especially shown to be the case in the North-West Provinces, where British power had

* Appendix A. of Deccan Ryots Commission's Report, pp. 154-180, minute of Lieutenant-Governor of the Punjab:—'That it is equally distasteful to the people of the North-Western Provinces, was sufficiently testified in 1857 by the scenes witnessed on the banks of the Eastern Jumna Canal by English refugees from Delhi—villages in flames in all directions, and their auction purchasers ejected and dispersed, while their women flung themselves into wells to escape dishonour.' Sir W. Muir also writes in 1859; —'I need hardly say that my opinion of the injury done by these sales has received grave confirmation from the events of the intervening period. The passing of landed estates into the hands of mere speculators, without any local influence or connection with the soil, was always regarded as a serious disadvantage. It ousted from their ancestral lands those who, by their natural position, could best manage them and be made instrumental in aiding the administration, and it substituted a set of men who were often unable even in times of peace to maintain themselves in secure possession, and for all administrative purposes were far less responsible and less useful proprietors. In addition to this, we have now had universal proof that the moment the authority of Government is suspended the old proprietors reassert their foregone rights and oust the upstart intruders.' (See Appendix IX.)

been longest established, and very few obstacles had been put in the way of sales.

The Board of Revenue's memorandum, drawn up on the statements made by various Settlement officers, concluded as follows:—'The land is beyond doubt passing into new hands, and at the ratio of the last thirty years, the whole of the country would be in the hands of non-agricultural classes in 150 years. . . . The village communities have suffered more than the talukdars. . . . The pressure of existing embarrassments, combined with an enhanced demand, will probably rather accelerate the rate of transfer among the communities during the next ten or twelve years.'

As regards the character of the new landowners, opinions appear to have differed, but there can be no doubt that a large amount of heartburning must have been the result of the transfers, especially when, as some settlement officers admitted, the pressure * of the State demand was the immediate cause.

It is clear, therefore, as a result of the stringent collection of the land-tax, especially if the assess-

* Thus, according to the Board's memorandum, quoted pages 53–58 in Appendix A., the settlement officer of Sháhjahánpur 'divides the pargamas into those which are (1) heavily, (2) moderately, (3) lightly assessed, and shows that the percentage of transfer, after eliminating disturbing causes in each, has severally been 24·5, 9·4, and 6.' A sold-up landowner is allowed in the North-Western Provinces to hold at a favourable rate sufficient land to support him. He thus becomes tenant of the land he formerly owned. Of course he cannot move away altogether, unless he is prepared to starve.

ment is heavy, and the baneful action of the civil courts in the matter of debt, the landowner is driven either to rack-rent his tenants or to mortgage and sell his land. The latter course is becoming more and more common in those parts of India where it has been found necessary to pass Acts to protect the tenants.

In the North-West Provinces, the Punjab and Central Provinces, a large number of tenants have what are called occupancy-rights; in Oudh these rights have hitherto only been given to ex-proprietors, but the Government reserves to itself the power of extending them, if rack-rents become common. Where such rights have been granted, the landlord's income, already in many cases curtailed by the State's demand, becomes still smaller, and litigation is greatly increased, as what was previously settled by custom is now decided by a suit in the rent court. However necessary such protection of tenants has been proved to be, its effect on the small landowner must not be ignored.

To sum up the general consequences of British rule as affecting the agricultural classes, it may be safely asserted that a powerful solvent has been suddenly introduced, disintegrating the whole fabric of social life. Some customs have been crystallised, others have been dissolved; classes that were at the top of the social scale are sinking to the bottom, and the once stable, though not inelastic, structures of society, have been subjected to severe shocks.

But beyond the power of the blows which are to be seen shattering the shell, the core of native life and thought remains for the most part intact, human nature asserting its distinctive privilege of hardening its heart in spite of repeated assaults. For the ever-present pressure of daily life, with its unchanging round of work and its alternating periods of rain and sunshine, seed-time and harvest, strengthens the intense conservatism of an illiterate population.*

> Das ganz
> Gemeine ist's, das ewig Gestrige,
> Was immer war und immer wiederkehrt,
> Und morgen gilt, weil's heute hat gegolten,
> Denn aus Gemeinem ist der Mensch gemacht,
> Und die Gewohnheit nennt er seine Amme.

The inhabitants of large cities may get their ideas modified by contact with Europeans and by

* In a rural district of 2,000 square miles, with a population of one million, there may be perhaps 120 schools, with 6,000 to 8,000 children on the books. The merest smattering of the three R's in the vernacular is all that is possible, except in one or two centre schools, where English may be learnt. On the other hand, the general intelligence of the peasantry is less exercised now than it used to be, by the village councils having been gradually shouldered out by the law courts. Hence the greatest stimulus to progress—discussion of public affairs—is withdrawn. It is now difficult, however desirable, to restore arbitration—*punchayets* to their former place in public estimation. The same is the case with the higher classes: they have few or no public duties to perform. Here and there a native is made an honorary or assistant magistrate, but the instances are not numerous. An aristocracy with no civil or military career soon becomes effeminate, especially in the East. In British territory the old families appear to be gradually going to the dogs, in spite of Encumbered Estates Acts.

the scraps of Western knowledge which they pick up in the town schools; but the villager remains absolutely untouched by such influences, except so far as they coerce him through the medium of the courts, in the shape of hostile and erratic forces.

It is this striking contrast between the changes imposed from without and the stability of the inner life —where it does not actually change for the worse— that creates a state of things fraught with enormous danger. We have shown the most complete tolerance to the different religious ideas of the natives, but we have treated with the utmost intolerance their social customs. The disruption of social bonds has fostered a litigious spirit, with its attendant spirit of lying. For, though strictly honourable to each other, when confronted by the public opinion of their village, as may be seen in the matter of debts, they will lie unblushingly in a court of law where they find an unfamiliar set of ideas in full force, and the rich man having the whip-hand of them. An experienced Oudh civilian writes: 'When I was trying cases in U, witnesses from Nepal never told a lie, those from the North of Oudh, where our courts were practically unknown, very seldom, and those from the North-West Provinces living only a few miles off, hardly ever told the truth.'

The sight of endless litigation is, no doubt, dear to the heart of the lawyer; it increases his importance, it fulfils all his expectations, but to everyone else it is a cause of sorrow. The simple-minded and thoughtless peasants use their rights like children use knives, only to cut themselves and others. This result, according to the legal mind, is proof of the desirability of giving them rights, but common sense tells us that it is proof of their unfitness for having edged tools given them, when their whole antecedents and surroundings are such that they cannot be expected to use them properly. 'Yes, but they will learn in time,' is the stereotyped answer. Have they learnt in provinces where British rule has been longest established? It is a notorious fact that in the North-West Provinces the results have been most disastrous to the peasantry. Is it likely that their characters, which are the outcome of their history, will change in the twinkling of an eye? The trump of doom is much more likely to sound first in their ears. 'Long before the people can be educated,' is the oft-repeated remark of the district officer, 'and the habits of improvidence, the growth of ages, cured, the land will have passed into the hands of a rapacious middle class who will rack-rent it and reduce the cultivators to slavery.'

In years of peace and plenty they may forget their grievances, but when a political crisis occurs like the Mutiny, or an economic disturbance like that in the Deccan, or a physical calamity like the recent terrible famine, it becomes plain to the most bigoted believer in the blessings of English rule that there is excessive friction going on, although the sound of it is lost. The idols of the market-place break to pieces the idols of the theatre, and the truth of the following remarks of Mr. Hume gets its full recognition:—'We have gone on elaborating in every branch highly organised systems of administration, which were alike beyond the wants and the wealth of our Indian fellow-subjects. So long as the masses of the population remained as poor, and therefore necessarily ignorant, as they still are, all that was needed was a rough system of patriarchal administration, a purified and somewhat systematised reproduction of the native rule that we replaced, a development of the then existing (now unfortunately almost extinct) system of self-government by juries, and a rigid repression of all crimes of violence. Under such a form of government, and it has existed for a time in almost every province we have acquired, the people have ever been more contented and better satisfied with their lot than under any of the more advanced and Europeanised forms that have later always displaced it.'

But although, from time to time, high officials admit that all this is true, yet experience shows that it is easy for a bureaucracy to go ahead in securing greater uniformity in administration,

> Sed revocare gradum
> Hoc opus, hic labor est.

The Deccan Ryots Relief Bill passed last year

in the Legislative Council, after great delay, is a hopeful sign for the future. But the difficulties which have attended this small measure of justice to rescue an impoverished peasantry, forbid us to expect that there will be much more movement in this direction, until some equally startling events like those which occurred in the Deccan have again given a check to the pitiless progress of the legislative Juggernaut car.

Twenty-seven years ago, Captain (now Sir G.) Wingate warned* the Bombay Government what would be the results of the procedure of the civil courts, and his prophecies have been fulfilled to the letter in the Bombay Presidency, and will be fulfilled elsewhere, if steps are not taken to prevent it.

The history of Jhansi, a district in the North-West Provinces, exhibits an exact repetition of

* Deccan Ryots Commission's Report, Appendix A., pages 79–98. 'This miserable struggle between debtor and creditor is thoroughly debasing to both. The creditor is made by it a grasping, hard-hearted oppressor; the debtor a crouching and false-hearted slave. It is disheartening to contemplate, and yet it would be weakness to conceal the fact that this antagonism of classes and degradation of the people, which is fast spreading over the land, is the work of our laws and our rule. The corruption and impoverishment of the mass of the people for the enriching of the few has already made lamentable advances in some districts, and is in progress in all; and the evil is clearly traceable, in my opinion, to the enormous power which the law places in the hands of the creditor.' The high prices of cotton during the American War, and high wages during railway construction, salved the sore places for the time.

the same sad course of events. Some years ago Sir W. Muir wrote as follows:—'I can conceive nothing more disastrous for the Jhansi division than to sanction a system which must end in reducing the powerful and turbulent proprietors of Jhansi into tenants at the will of a body of non-resident speculators, whose only object will be to squeeze out of them the highest return for their money.' It is now a notorious fact, to which the Anglo-Indian Press is frequently calling attention, that the present state of Jhansi is exactly that which Sir W. Muir anticipated with horror. Who is to blame?* Chiefly the Civil Procedure Code and Revenue system, utterly unsuited to the character of the landowners and to the special requirements of a district where a periodical deficiency in the rainfall, and the spread of a noxious grass weed, make the yield of the soil very uncertain.

It seems that something will at last be done

* It is useless to repeat charges which I have heard made on good authority against individuals for their share in this disastrous result, for owing to the rapid change of officials, and the number of persons who have to deal with any measure, it is well nigh impossible to fix any responsibility for any single act. Where there is no powerful Press or inquisitive Parliament to bring matters home, the public can always be put off. Who will ever be proved responsible for the recent financial fiasco? When I was in India I was astonished to hear so many charges of want of truthfulness in high places. I suppose, like the native in an English law court, high officials get rather demoralised from the absence of a bracing public opinion. Human nature is very identic when exposed to temptation. 'Tush! tush! mortal men, mortal men!'

with this too often pigeon-holed problem, as a Bill, moving on the lines of the Deccan Ryots Relief Bill, has been recently introduced in the Viceroy's Legislative Council.

But although the indebtedness of the peasantry in the Deccan and Jhansi districts has excited especial attention, there is every reason to believe that the same cankerworm is gnawing at the vitals of the social organism in every part of British India. The symptoms may vary in acuteness, but the evidence collected by the Deccan Riots Commission proves that the disease is co-extensive with our administration.

The Punjab is generally supposed to be in the most flourishing state, but in the debate on the Deccan Relief Bill the Lieutenant-Governor said that in that province 'there was many a peasant proprietor whose condition is very much the same as that of the Deccan ryot;' and he went so far as to assert that the circumstances leading to the Bill were of general prevalence throughout India. 'The cultivator has to be protected against the Government as much as against the usurer.' He also added that 'the stringency of our regulations, the rigorous demand of Government,' force the former into the latter's hands. The justice of this accusation was not denied by such a staunch champion of bureaucratic indifferentism as Sir John Strachey, while the Legal Member of Council was alone bold enough to take up the cudgels in defence of the blessings of Benthamite jurisprudence.

Effectual Relief Bills must not only deal with the action of the Civil Procedure Code, but must modify the relentless rigour of the revenue system, and allow more discretion to the local authorities in the collection of the land-tax. It is the State that plays the part of a plundering army, while it throws all the blame on the camp followers, who take the opportunity for petty pillage which is so freely offered them. It is right to see that justice is done between the usurer and his victim, but the State ought itself to set the example. A Liberal ministry which has brought forward a Bill to restrain Irish landlords in evictions for rent, might consistently urge the Indian Government to show more leniency in its exactions of land-revenue.

CHAPTER IV.

IN spite of the admitted defects of our judicial machinery and the disastrous failure of some of our codes, the task of law-making is allowed to proceed as merrily as ever. In 1875, when Lord Salisbury with his usual self-assurance* pressed the Indian Government to sanction the resumption of the process of codification which had been lately suspended, Lord Northbrook's Council recorded an emphatic protest against introducing *new* laws—the inevitable effect of codification in a country like India—faster than it could bear. The despatch went on as follows: 'The people of this country do not accept change readily. They have no constitutional machinery for making their sentiments known, so that we may be long in finding out how they are affected by changes in laws; but they are more or less unsettled by every change, and if the change happens to be an important one the unsettlement is lasting. It is therefore more prudent not to make many changes simultaneously, because the inevitable disturbances resulting from

* Despatch of Secretary of State for India, published in *Gazette of India*, February 15, 1879.

each may be too much in the aggregate, and also because it is desirable to know something of the working of one before bringing on another. Indeed, in our judgment, India is not the country into which any large body of law, either actually or virtually new, can prudently be introduced except slowly and cautiously.'

They also pointed out the great labour caused to the small staff of officials who carry on the business of the country in having to learn new laws, and expressed their opinion that the consolidation and simplification of existing laws was the most desirable work for the legislative department for some time to come. They concluded by saying that the* Civil Procedure Code then in hand would involve several controversies of considerable difficulty, and that codification might wait for a more convenient season.

But with the appearance on the scene of Lord Lytton as Viceroy and Mr. Whitley Stokes as Legal Member of Council, Lord Salisbury returned to the charge. In a despatch, dated January 20,

* It is well known that Lord Macaulay's famous Criminal Code, after its final revision by Sir Barnes Peacock, has hardly required a single amendment. The same care was taken with Sir J. Stephen's Criminal Procedure and Evidence Code. But the Civil Procedure Code seems to have been hurried on, and is now undergoing a thorough revision. But as if these changes were not enough to worry the hard-worked judicial staff, the legislative department has set to work on substantive law, and Mr. Whitley Stokes is desirous also of remodelling the Criminal Procedure Code. See Appendix X.

1876, the Secretary of State, with his characteristic obliviousness of anybody else's opinions except his own, asserts that 'all objections to codification are altogether outweighed by the vast practical usefulness which has recommended this method to most of the nations of Europe.' And in view of the fact that an Indian Law Commission had been appointed in India in 1833, and in England in 1853 and 1861, he 'is of opinion that the completion of a Code of Law is an accepted policy which cannot now be abandoned without great detriment to the people and serious discredit to the Indian Government. He forbears therefore (this is very characteristic of the noble Marquis's Indian despatches) from dwelling on the reasons which might be adduced in favour of that policy if its continuance were now under discussion.'

On the utterly unstatesmanlike tone of this despatch, its absolute disregard for the enormous difference between India and Europe, its complete contentment with the light of inner consciousness, it is needless to comment. Nobody expects anything else from a Marquis whom Providence has sent into the world to continue the interrupted policy of the Elizabethan age. But that any Viceroy should give his consent to the initiation of a gigantic social revolution is almost beyond belief. The only explanation is that foreign affairs became too urgent for Lord Lytton to keep in check an aspiring barrister, and that Mr. Whitley Stokes is responsible for the wonderful despatch which was sent in reply to Lord Salisbury's peremptory orders.

The scheme sketched out is as follows: The chapter of the Indian Civil Code treating of contract is to be supplemented by codes on the following subjects: (*a*) sale of immovable property, mortgages, exchanges, leases; (*b*) insurance; (*c*) carriers; (*d*) negotiable instruments; (*e*) bottomry, respondentia, and the other liens on movables, with certain exceptions. Then are to follow codes on certain personal relations, such as those between master and servant, parent and child, on trusts, servitudes or easements, boundaries, alluvion and diluvion. Lastly, torts are to be dealt with. It is significantly stated, by the way, that 'such a scheme would perhaps enable us to make some urgently needed social reforms, without the risk of exciting popular opposition, and that it would assuredly diffuse among the people of India a more accurate knowledge of their rights and duties than they will attain if their law is left in the present state' (i.e. partially codified, but mostly left to the interpretation of the Local Courts, guided by local usage, with the assistance of analogies from English law).

The light in which this project of speculative radicalism is viewed by practical statesmen of unusually wide experience in Indian matters, may be seen in a minute recorded by Lord Northbrook's Council, consisting of Lord Napier, Sir A. Hobhouse, Sir W. Muir, Sir A. Eden, Sir A. Arbuthnot, and Sir A. Clarke.

'We are aware that from a lawyer's point of view a code on the subject of tortious acts or wrongs would be a valuable addition to a body of written law. But we doubt very much whether it would benefit Indian society. It would perhaps be more effectual in suggesting kinds of litigation now very rare, if not wholly unknown in India, than in removing difficulties actually felt in practice. In fact, on many subjects rights have not become sufficiently settled to afford a basis for codified laws of wrongs. In some cases (as, for instance, the somewhat delicate subject of claims to privacy), a right has been found to exist in one territory, and not elsewhere. To propose a uniform law on such a subject would lead to much difficulty.'

With such an emphatic warning it is superfluous to point out the dangerous* spirit of innovation which would evidently attend the working of the above codification scheme. And yet it is a notorious fact that the Legislative Department is now preparing to impose on India, with all its diversity of race, creed, and civilisation, a body of uniform Civil Law, in spite of the emphatic protests of Local Governments.† As the *Pioneer*,

* In reply to the invitation of the Indian Army Commission, to state what were the elements of disorder and sources of popular discontent or danger in their respective provinces, 'more than one of the local authorities so questioned have deliberately replied tha the unsympathetic legislation of recent years is a source of danger.' —*Pioneer Mail*, April 22, 1880.

† Sir Henry Maine, in an appendix to his volume on *Village*

in a recent article on the subject, well asked, 'What would be thought of a statesman who tried to impose the Code Napoleon on the whole of Europe—Russia and Turkey included?' And yet such an undertaking would be a mere whipping with rods compared with the chastisement by scorpions which fanatical lawyers are prepared to inflict on India.

Owing to the vehement outcries of the local authorities and the Anglo-Indian Press, a Law Commission,* consisting of Mr. Whitley Stokes as

Communities, and Sir James Stephen, in his chapter on 'Legislation in India,' contributed to Dr. Hunter's *Life of Lord Mayo*, agree in saying that during their respective terms of office the utmost deference was shown to the local Governments before any fresh enactments were brought forward. This has not been the case as far as the codification scheme is concerned. The increased charge for stationery and printing during the last few years must be, in part, the result of the codification scheme. Countless copies of proposed codes, with hundreds of sections, have been circulated during the last year among district officers to receive the benefit of their criticism.

* Why were not some experienced administrators placed on the Commission so as to criticise the lucubrations of the legal mind? Of course, the president and his assessors passed a vote of confidence in themselves. In an Article which appeared in the *Pall Mall* of April 16, and which seemed to emanate from some member of the commission, codification is said to be 'opposed on one side by the blind jealousy of legal practitioners, who have accustomed themselves to existing disorder till they think it natural, and the vague dislike of change which expresses the confused scepticism of common sense, on the other hand, by the refined scepticism of over-subtle theorists.' This gives a wholly false idea of the real grounds of opposition. Mr. Whitley Stokes appears not to have the slightest idea of the peasant life of India, his experience being confined to Calcutta and Simla. Each part of India would require its own

President and two other Indian judges as ordinary members, was last year appointed at Simla, to consider the whole scheme of codification, and their report was issued some months ago. Its appearance was hailed with uproarious shouts of laughter. The pompous grandiloquence of its legal and philosophical dicta, the confident assumption of Divine omniscience as regards the present and future needs of India, are enough to stamp it as the work of men who are possessed by a craze.

Let us select one of the *purpurei panni* of the new Gospel of Law: 'It is of the nature of the human mind and character to be deeply impressed by an orderly development of consequences from received principles, even when that development takes a course different from what unaided instinct and the first rude necessities of practice have suggested. Thus, by timely legislation, taking just account of existing legal conditions as an outgrowth of the past and a necessary basis of the future, we may save the community many painful experiences, put it into possession of the fruits of others' labours and pains, and hasten by whole generations its entry into the great procession of the nations towards an uniformity of laws founded on uni-

code, as is the case with its Rent Acts. 'No law should be made,' wrote Sir James Stephen in Mr. Hunter's *Life of Lord Mayo*, 'till it is distinctly perceived and felt to be necessary. No one can admit more fully or feel more strongly than I the evils and dangers of mere speculative legislation in India.'

formity in the conception of right and of the essential elements of human welfare.'

These be brave words. For the future, law is not to be the outcome of a nation's life, bone of its bone and flesh of its flesh, but a sort of dry nurse ('I spy a great peard under his muffler') with an unlimited supply of forcing food and cotton wool to accelerate its growth and to prevent any bruises. Might not Providence be dispensed with now that the lawyers are ready to take its place, and a liturgy of law be drawn up beginning 'let us codify'?

Of course, the analogy of Europe's absorption of Roman law is brought forward, but the difference between the East and West, between one century and twenty centuries, between the sudden imposition of law wholesale at the point of a foreign bayonet and the gradual assimilation of portions of the same carefully selected by friendly brain-power, is hardly mentioned at all, or is mentioned only to be set aside. General admissions are made of the fact that, on the one hand, Hindoo society is a living body, with its own laws of unmeasured antiquity, 'its religion interwoven with those laws,' and that any outsider must experience great difficulty in entering into the feelings of Hindoo or Mussulman; that, on the other, in its external conditions, owing to the introduction of foreign rule, it is in a state of flux. But such admissions are of no use if the legal mind still thinks itself able to determine its future evolution.

When Lord Cranbrook became Secretary of State for India, he determined to check the impetus which his predecessor so unwisely gave to the tyrannical action of the Legislative Department. In his despatch of Sept. 5, 1878, he expressed 'his strong opposition to any scheme for compressing the completion of the Civil Code within a period of five years or any other definite time.' His reasons were, that 'any such attempt will tend to produce haste and consequent imperfection in an undertaking which, before all things, requires deliberate care. The branches of law which remain to be codified are, on the whole, more complex than those which have been already declared in chapters of the Code, and the difficulties of harmonising* them with the feelings and usages of the people will be unusually great.'

But although Lord Cranbrook has advised caution, yet some other Secretary of State will perhaps again encourage this patent scheme for creating discontent in India. Bundles of codes will be showered broadcast like bales of cotton, in the belief that the native can as easily appreciate English ideas of right as he can appropriate Manchester piece goods.

* It is interesting to read the appendices to the Indian Law Commission's Report, and to see how the doctors differ when they come to the practical application of their principles. They almost come to loggerheads on the question of local usages as regards easements, diluvion, and alluvion. It would also appear from certain remarks, that Sir H. Maine and Sir J. Stephen have forwarded some severe criticisms, but they are not published in full.

We have at last learnt that India is very poor; we have still to learn that it is very primitive, if gauged by the standard of Western ideas. Those who think that with the assistance of a legal go-cart, put together in the most scientific fashion, any country can be safely transported over the yawning gulf of centuries, must be utterly blind to the lessons of the past. Indeed, although now-a-days such terms as stages of civilisation and the like make up a great part of the popular philosophy of history, it may be doubted whether they at all adequately account for the radical divergences of the East and West. 'Time is no more to a Hindoo than to a sitting hen,' was a remark recently made by a shrewd American traveller. Hearken, O ye narrow-minded lawyers!

However desirable it may be to accelerate the movement of Orientals, yet it is impossible to do so except to a very small extent. We cannot suddenly place one animal organism in the surroundings adapted to another of a wholly different species without endangering its life; still less can we do this in the case of a highly-organised animal like man. Each type of human nature must be left to create its social and economical 'medium' in virtue of its own vital force; it can no more live in one created for it than the snail can live in a manufactured shell. A certain amount of guidance is all that is possible, and that guidance must come from those who have studied its inner being, and are therefore able to offer it the mental food which it is capable of assimilating. Viewed from without, the formation of man's social environment may seem to be independent of his mind and character; but closer observation proves that outer and inner are correlative terms. Foreign ideas must become familiar before they can be utilised for the furtherance of man's estate. All history teaches us that sudden changes introduced into any society without intelligent co-operation on its part are sure to prove fatal to the true and permanent interests of that society. Moved by the instinct of self-preservation, Russia has for some time past been struggling to free herself of alien influences, and China fears their introduction.

Every English statesman to whom the destinies of India are entrusted ought, when tempted by the spirit of rash innovation, to take to heart the warning words of Schiller's 'Wallenstein':—

> Du willst die Macht
> Die ruhig, sicher thronende erschüttern,
> Die in verjährt geheiligtem Besitz
> In der Gewohnheit fest gegründet ruht,
> Die an der Völker frommem Kinderglauben
> Mit tausend zähen Wurzeln sich befestigt.

Surely the scandalous results of English rule in Ireland ought to make us hesitate before we sanction the same procedure in India. The forcible imposition of English codes and courts, of

English land-tenures, the destruction of Irish trade in deference to Liverpool and Bristol, have not been so very advantageous to the former country that with light hearts we should gird ourselves for the same destructive work in the latter. Although we Englishmen have never yet shown much appreciation for 'Saviours of Society' amongst ourselves, yet we seem to think that Providence has intended that our countrymen should play this part as regards others. Let our Irish difficulties warn us to 'put a hook in the nose' of men like Mr. Whitley Stokes.

CHAPTER V.

As if the fuel already given, and soon to be added to in the shape of codes, shaped in the most scientific fashion, was not enough to kindle the flames of discontent, Sir J. Strachey, in 1877, added certain explosive materials, drawn from the magazine of direct taxation. It is true that the solemn plausibility with which they were again ushered into use, and the slightly different colour with which they were painted, at first seemed to justify the expectation that they might not prove so dangerous as before. But experience has shown that all the arguments which have been adduced against them under the name of income-tax are equally valid under their new name of license-tax.

In 1869, when an income-tax was imposed, the following opinions* were expressed in Council: 'The Maharajah of Jeypore openly declared that of all modes of direct taxation the income-tax was the most ill suited to this country and the most opposed to the feelings of the people.' . . . 'The

* The following quotations appeared originally in the *Calcutta Review* 1872, and were requoted by the *Pioneer* of November 25, 1879. (See Appendix XI.)

late Sir H. Durand followed in the same strain.' Towards the close of 1869, after a great outcry in the English and Native Press, 'district officers, finding themselves at last consulted, expressed their almost unanimous opinion regarding the impossibility of justly distributing direct taxation.' In the ensuing debate in Council, Messrs. Chapman, Bullen, Smith, and Cowie, the two latter non-officials, expressed in the strongest way their objection against such unsuitable taxation.

But the debate of March 1871 is the *locus classicus* on the subject. Mr. Robinson, from Madras, said that 'Anyone practically acquainted with the working of the income-tax knew that the whole thing, from one end of the country to the other, was an unseemly and demoralising wrangle between the lower orders of Government officials and the people of *all* classes. For from interested motives the challenge was carried far below the classes intended to be taxed, and exemption fees were levied by threats far and wide.' Mr. Inglis—afterwards Chief Commissioner of Oudh—said that 'There was probably no member of this Council who had had better opportunities than he for forming an opinion of this tax. He had to assess it as collector, to hear appeals against it as commissioner, and latterly to look after the assessment of the whole of the North-Western Provinces as a member of the Board of Revenue; and he had no hesitation in saying, in the words used by the Local Taxation

Committee assembled last year in the North-West, when speaking of the income-tax, that it was a tax odious to the people and odious to the officers who had to assess and collect it. . . . The area of the districts was so large, and the population so great, that it was impossible for any collector to make the assessments himself. He was consequently compelled to employ a lot of underpaid natives to prepare lists of the persons liable to assessment, and had to rely on information which he well knew to be untrustworthy. . . . He felt that he was working in the dark; that with the best intention and the most earnest desire to do right, he was probably every day committing the most frightful injustice.' He then went on to answer the plea, in favour of the income-tax, put forward by Sir R. Temple—that it was absurd to call a tax unpopular which fell on only one in three hundred of the population. 'It might be true that only one in three hundred of the people paid income-tax to Government, but it was equally true that of the two hundred and ninety-nine remaining, at least one-half were subjected to the most oppressive and vexatious inquisition and extortion. . . . It was, he believed, no exaggeration to say that for every man who paid income-tax to Government twenty paid to get off, and that for every rupee paid into the Treasury another was paid to subordinate native officials. . . . Everywhere throughout the country the tax was demoralising to the people;

everywhere false returns were sent in; everywhere the trading classes were beginning to keep two sets of books.'

In consequence of this strong speech, Lord Mayo ordered district officers to be asked for their opinions, and Sir W. Muir's Government, in forwarding their replies, which 'were, broadly speaking, at one with Mr. Inglis,' wrote as follows: 'So much his Honour may say without any hesitation, that in the course of a long service in India he has never before witnessed anything approaching the popular discontent created by the income-tax during the last two years.'

The only reply which Sir J. Strachey gave, and now gives, is that these abuses are due to maladministration.* But how is it possible for an English officer, with the aid of two or three subordinates in a district of about one million persons, spread over about 2,000 square miles, to prevent corruption and oppression? This question has been frequently asked by district officers, and *no answer has ever been given.*

It was, therefore, in the teeth of all experience

* I have been out in camp with a civilian while he was assessing the license-tax, and have seen what disagreeable work it is for all parties. Unless one is willing to make domiciliary visits, the only check on the lists sent in by native underlings is to get together the leading men of each place, and ask them questions about their neighbours' incomes, &c. Very often you find yourself playing into the hands of somebody's enemy. Friendly converse becomes impossible, grim suspicion filling everyone's heart.

that Sir J. Strachey imposed the license-tax, which was practically much the same as an income-tax, except in the matter of grades.* For two years it was levied, for the most part, from those who had an income of 200 rupees, but in Bengal it touched incomes of over 100 rupees. But this is not all. In spite of the solemn preamble of the License-Tax Act that the money would be used for famine insurance purposes, and after a distinct declaration in the Budget of 1878 (paragraph 38) that 'it would be in opposition to the pledges given by the Government and the instructions of the Secretary of State to undertake any fiscal measures of reform, if they would involve fresh taxation, and this prohibition must be applied to the future as well as to the present,' the Government partially abolished the cotton duties, thereby immediately losing £250,000 of revenue, and endangering the retention of the remaining £600,000.

* To show what a terrible amount of friction was caused by the license-tax, I will quote the statistics of Bengal, 'ab uno disce omnes.' Out of a total assessment of 4,822,851 rupees, 20.26,111 had to be remitted; 130,287 were not recoverable. A staff of 264 native officials had to assess a population of over 60 millions—i.e. each official had to pick, out of a population of 230,000 residing in 680 villages, those who were liable to the tax. Is it possible to prevent injustice? It was supposed that the hateful inquisitions which took place under the income-tax would be avoided under a license-tax, but practically, whenever any attempt was made to get a fair assessment, officers have been forced to carry them out. At Lucknow, an English civilian had to be specially appointed for the purpose, and spent days in the native bazaars performing the most disagreeable work. (See Appendix XI.)

A new issue is therefore raised. Is direct or indirect taxation the most suited to India?

The powerful objections against all direct * taxation, that goes low enough to be very profitable, have been already mentioned, and when they are compared with the great ease and cheapness of collecting the customs duties, it becomes clear that if revenue must be raised (and everyone admits there ought to be an annual surplus to fall back on) the argument is wholly on the side of raising them by the latter method.

Is, then, India to be deprived of this most suitable source of revenue, because, owing to the conditions of her agricultural and industrial life, customs duties are slightly, and that indirectly, protective? Is one of the least economically advanced

* The license-tax now yields £515,000; the land-cess of 1878 £509,000, so that the two combined are rather more than the £800,000 odd yielded two years ago by the cotton duties. Superficially, they may be regarded as alternative schemes, but they differ essentially in the discontent which they excite. If the rest of the cotton duties go, the remainder of the customs duties will not be worth the trouble of collection. Of course, there is not now the same objection to the license-tax when it does not touch incomes below 500 rupees, though an income-tax on professional and salaried classes ought obviously to be combined with it. But as an alternative to indirect taxation, it is open to most serious objections, especially when the money so raised is not applied to its proper purpose. Although only the trifling sum of 5,069 rupees is, according to the official report, said to have been spent in 1878 on the license-tax establishments of the North-Western Province and Oudh, yet, as every official well knows, the time of hard-worked English magistrates and native revenue-officials, was for weeks taken up with assessments, and their proper work had to be scamped or postponed.

countries in the world to be forced to go beyond the most advanced, and lose all its income from import duties? It is perfectly absurd to maintain this paradoxical proposition. It is only obstinate dogmatists like the Marquis of Salisbury and Sir J. Strachey, or interested parties like Lancashire cotton-spinners that would venture to say that they are considering the true interests of India in forcing her to have free ports. It cannot be for a moment supposed that in a wealthy country like England, if it were found impossible to put on any duties which were not slightly protective, any financier would dare to dispense with the customs revenue. Why should an English Ministry force it on India? If India were polled on the question of direct versus indirect taxation, there is not a shadow of doubt as to the answer.* Once let the remainder of the cotton duties be abolished, and where is there any financial reserve except in a hateful income- or license-tax? † At some critical time, when it ought to be the desire of every statesman to enlist the

* Sir J. Strachey admits in the last financial statement that so far from there being any direct protection, Lancashire manufacturers are now importing a class of goods not made by the Indian mills, and yet free from duty.

† If, owing in part to loss of customs revenue, the English treasury has to make advances to India, is not this taxing the community for the benefit of Lancashire—i.e., giving a bounty? Is not this practically protection?

The cotton duties are now entirely levied on the finer class of goods—i.e., they are paid by the well-to-do classes—i.e., those very persons whom it is so difficult otherwise to get at.

sympathies of India, will it be wise to cause nothing but 'wailing and gnashing of teeth?' 'Taxing,' said Burke, 'is an easy business. Any projector can contrive new impositions; any bungler can add to the old. But is it altogether wise to have no other bounds to your impositions than the patience of those who are to bear them?' The force of this protest is a thousand-fold increased when India is the country in question.

In 1875 Lord Northbrook, in reviewing the proposal to abolish the cotton duties, wrote as follows:—

'India is a country in which there is but little choice of new sources of taxation; it would be difficult to replace a large amount of revenue except by an excise duty on tobacco or some kind of direct taxation. I am satisfied that such a change would not be desirable even in a financial point of view. The army of tax-gatherers on low pay, which would be let loose over the country to collect a new excise, would probably involve a larger charge to the Government than the cost of collecting the customs duties; and, what is of more importance, by the imposition of a new excise duty or by direct taxation under the best arrangements that could be made to levy either, the people of India would, in my opinion, have to pay a larger sum than they would gain by the reduced cost of the articles which would be affected by the abolition of our customs duties. But this is not all; I have no hesitation in asserting that the political evil of giving up our customs duties, or a large part of them, and imposing fresh taxation in their place, would be great. Whatever may be the objection to customs duties, they possess the advantage of being collected easily and paid without pressure. These advantages are of peculiar importance in India, where new taxes are peculiarly liable to occasion popular discontent. To substitute direct taxes or new excise duties for the customs duties which are now imposed upon foreign goods, seems to me a policy which would be contrary to the interests and people of India, and which no statesman with a knowledge of India and a sense of responsibility could be found to propose.'

All such weighty considerations have been recklessly thrust aside by a finance-minister who, as he once informed the Viceroy's Council, has been endowed with the power of 'dipping into the future and seeing the untaxed wares of the world pouring into the free ports of India.' Fired by such a magnificent vision, he never appears to have asked himself the homely question whether, after all the 'plundering and blundering' of local cesses and license-taxes, the peasantry would have any means to avail themselves of the privilege thus thrust upon them.

CHAPTER VI.

THE above account of the normal working of the revenue system and civil codes, and the abnormal worrying of recent financial measures, is sufficient to show that the mildest Hindoo has reason to feel some irritation and to count the cost—to him—of the brightest jewel in the British Crown.

To speak of British rule in India as an experiment unparalleled in the history of the world is to indulge in an unwarrantable euphemism. Our analogies should be drawn from the dissecting room rather than the laboratory. For our present method of procedure entails the incessant vivisection of thousands of human beings, whose sufferings no one ought to contemplate except with intense compassion. It is true that, owing to the frequent change of the operators from place to place, and the interposition of Boards and Bureaux which deaden the sound, the cries of the creatures whose flesh is cut, do not often penetrate to the ears of those who have dealt out the instruments of anguish. But this silence only increases the victims' agonies, for they are not soothed by the anæsthetic of friendly sympathy. It is to be hoped that good will come out of them for generations yet unborn, but the process is very painful, as wrought out by the energy of unimaginative Englishmen. We are very apt to forget the immense differences between the West and East, the former with its master movement towards the realisation of human freedom and the subjugation of natural forces, the latter with its placid acquiescence in its already attained position and powers, its 'mit leben, mit leiden, mit geniessen das Dasein der Welt.' In India these two divergent civilisations have come into sudden collision, and it is the onerous duty of English statesmanship to work out their reconciliation, to harmonise the spirit of progress and the spirit of fixity, but it must be the work of centuries, if it is to be permanent.

Having assumed this high responsibility we cannot, as a nation, withdraw from it; frightful anarchy would be the inevitable result. We have introduced rights which popular sentiment does not recognise, and if British force was withdrawn, agrarian outbreaks would take place throughout the whole continent. Irish anti-rent agitations would be completely overshadowed by Indian anti-usury risings.

Our primary duty in India is the preservation of order, whereby the country may be able, if such a thing is possible, to strike out a fresh line of development. At present there is great danger that beneath the appearance of universal peace we are sowing the seeds of widespread war, and a war of the most fatal sort, because intestine in the strongest sense of the word. It will be a sad paradox if the boasted pioneers of civilisation, after driving out the spirit of disorder, end their task by bringing it back into its old habitation, swept and garnished, for its permanent abode.

If we would avoid such a catastrophe it is necessary to show a much greater regard for the feelings and ideas of those whom we rule with such an iron hand. What seems to us very small progress may yet be to them a great event.

> Say not a 'small event,' why 'small'?
> Costs it more pain that this ye call
> A 'great event' should come to pass
> Than that? Untwine me from the mass
> Of deeds which make up life one deed,
> Power shall fall short in or exceed.'

It is less science and more sympathy that is required of Anglo-Indian statesmen.

And even an enlightened self-interest ought to warn us of the political dangers which must threaten our empire if the irritation, not to say exasperation, which is known to exist, should be able to make itself felt on any large scale. Mr. Hunter and others may remind us of the terrible scenes of bloodshed which marked the course of the Persian and Afghan invaders during the last century, and which we now prevent. A very similar defence is put by Thucydides in the mouth of the apologist of the Athenian Empire :—'Our subjects,' he says, 'put up with worse treatment than this under the Persian;' but he appends the further terse, but pregnant remark:—'Yet our rule is held to be severe, and naturally so, for subjects always feel the weight of the present.'

However great have been the sufferings of India in times past, they are gradually fading from the memory of the illiterate masses. Moreover, the upper classes under Mahomedan rule* to a great extent performed the part of buffers which eased off the collision of the foreign conqueror and the conquered peasantry; and native customs were for the most part maintained. But our policy takes away all these mollifying influences. A succession of far-reaching changes, destructive of ancient families and breaking up at every point the immemorial usages of a venerable social system, has made the native thoroughly suspicious as regards our ultimate intentions.

'A year or two† ago an inquiry was made of our most intelligent officers in the East, not as to

* In the introduction to the *Oudh Gazetteer* it is pointed out that 'The old Muhammadan despotism never interfered in the civil disputes of its subjects . . . they were arranged when between men of the same class by caste arbitration boards, otherwise by the order of the local chieftain . . . All that is now altered. One of these instruments, the chieftain, has been entirely superseded; and if men of different castes disagree they are compelled to resort to the arbitrament of our tribunals. The decisions of caste panchayets are weakened by the existence of a co-ordinate and sometimes superseding jurisdiction.

† *Physics and Politics*, by W. Bagehot.

whether the English Government were really doing good in the East, but as to whether the natives of India themselves thought we were doing good; to which, in a majority of the cases, the officers who were the best authority answered thus: No doubt you are giving the Indians many great benefits. You give them continued peace, free trade, the right to live as they like, subject to the laws; in these points and others they are far better off than they ever were; but still they cannot make you out. What puzzles them is your constant disposition to change, or as you call it, improvement. Their own life in every detail being regulated by ancient usage, they cannot comprehend a policy which is always bringing something new: they do not a bit believe that the desire to make them comfortable and happy is the root of it; they believe, on the contrary, that you are aiming at something which they do not understand—that you mean to "take away their religion;" in a word that the end and object of all these continual changes is to make Indians not what they are and what they like to be, but something new and different from what they are, and what they would not like to be.'

When this sense of the insecurity of all which lies nearest to the native's heart becomes deepened and the belief in our irresistible might grows weaker, we shall have to prepare for a desperate struggle, the issue of which no one could venture to foresee.

India is not as yet a burden on this country—far from it. Although the pagoda trees of her princes may no longer be shaken by a few lucky or unscrupulous individuals, her peasantry still pour riches into the English nation's lap. But if the Indian Government by its contemptuous disregard of popular feeling is allowed to goad the whole country into rebellion, India may soon become a burden too heavy to be borne. For even if we proved ultimately victorious, yet we should find it impossible to recoup ourselves, as after the mutiny, for the expenditure incurred. Increased taxation would be a serious set-off against the advantages of an Indian Empire, and orators like Mr. Bright would find a firm basis—at present wanting—for their declamations.

Nor should we, as a nation, have the heart to bear these sacrifices, when no longer sustained by the proud consciousness of a great mission. For we should have been weighed in the scales and found wanting—wanting in that very quality which is essential to a truly imperial people, the power of gradually breathing the spirit of its civilisation into the races which it has conquered. This alone can be the true justification of empire, and the absence of it its effectual condemnation. The phrase *Pax Romana* is the eternal glory of Roman imperialism, that of *Pestis Britannica* may yet be the undying disgrace of the British Empire in India.

In order to avert such a verdict at the bar of

History, it is necessary to bring the weight of a well-informed public opinion to bear on the action of the Indian Government. The present moment is not an unsuitable time for a return to less revolutionary methods of procedure.* Famine, war, and an ill-paid and therefore discontented native army are necessarily conducive to great searchings of heart, and the most optimistic official must feel some qualms for the future. No more beneficial task could be undertaken by a really Liberal Government than that of striving to instil its life-giving principles into the dry bones of a bureaucratic despotism. It may not be possible to establish any form of representative government which shall give direct expression to India's wishes, but it is possible to pay a greater attention to the well-known sentiments of the country as indirectly revealed through experienced English officers. Public opinion in India must necessarily grow in strength with the increase of communication, and

* It is high time that the state of the native troops should be looked into. The Indian press is continually calling attention to the difficulty of getting recruits, owing to the low pay offered. According to the *Friend of India*, an inquiry a few years ago into the condition of the native army, showed that whereas in 1848 the cost of a month's living was two rupees, four annas, in 1875 it was five rupees, eight annas, or more than double, while the pay remained the same—i.e. seven rupees a month, and eight and a half rupees when marching. No one denies that the native troops have behaved splendidly in the Afghan War, in spite of bad treatment in the shape of pay stopped for boots &c., want of warm clothing at the beginning of the war and hard work throughout.

each act of the Government will be considered by a larger number of critics. It rests with us to alienate or conciliate the popular will, which we cannot suppress, though we may ignore it.

The Mutiny of 1857 is supposed to have been the child of fear as much as of hate. The native saw his well-known world threatened with destruction, and he rose against us in a panic of self-preserving energy. And yet, regardless of this warning, the Indian Government has moved on, especially during the last few years, seemingly bent on making history repeat itself on a larger scale. When its measures have been so suggestive of seditious thoughts, it has done well to pass a Press Act to restrain seditious language. Delhi assemblages, imperial proclamations, and rhetorical blandishments are worse than meaningless in the absence of straightforwardness, good faith, and justice. Lord Lytton's home-policy was vitiated by too great a love of diplomatic finesse and too implicit a trust in a fascinating finance-minister. By the poetic pipings of his literary genius he led India's 'sucking children to play by the hole of the asp,' and he has himself got the credit of the latter's venomous bites. It is to be hoped that the necessary antidotes may be plentifully furnished by Lord Ripon to the feverish body politic, and that the character of his administration may be summed up in the simple but suggestive words of Scripture, 'the land had rest.'

APPENDICES.

APPENDIX I.

The Viceroy's Administrative Council consists of:—

1. The Viceroy.

2. The Commander-in-Chief as extraordinary member.

3. Six ordinary members of Council, of whom three must be members either of the civil or of the military service in India, and one a barrister of five years' standing.* No special qualification is required for the Financial or Public Works member. Each of these members has charge of a department.

The Legislative Council consists of all the above, and

4. The Governor, Lieutenant-Governor, or Chief Commissioner of the Province in which the Council sits for the time being, generally, therefore, of Bengal or the Punjab.

5. Not less than six, nor more than twelve, additional members, of whom one half must be non-official.

The Governors of Bombay and Madras have each Administrative Councils, consisting of two civilian members and one military, and Legislative Councils consisting of the above members, and eight additional members,

* Office now in abeyance.

some of whom are natives. The Administrative Councils are supposed to be necessitated by the fact that the Governors may be destitute of Indian experience.

The Lieutenant-Governor of Bengal has also a Legislative Council.

The other provinces have no Councils.

The Viceregal Legislative Council tends more and more to conduct the legislation of the whole country. There is very little *bonâ fide* discussion in it, as the Viceroy practically secures a majority before introducing any measure. He has also the power of over-riding his Council when he considers 'the safety, tranquillity, or interests of the British possessions in India essentially affected.'

APPENDIX II.

As Professor Fawcett has pointed out in his 'Indian Finance,' the entire revenue of India, with the exception of £504,208, is derived from the six following sources: land, opium, salt, excise, customs, and stamps, their net receipts in an average year being as follows:—

Land	£17,352,541
Opium	6,280,813
Salt	5,816,178
Excise on spirits and drugs .	2,432,352
Customs	2,289,115
Stamps	2,742,362

Total between 37 and 38 million pounds sterling. It is much higher just now. Of these opium is not a tax.

It is very difficult to ascertain the increase of taxation

during any long period, because the form of keeping the accounts has been changed from time to time, and the census has only been fairly accurate during recent dates. However it is possible to mention some admitted instances of fresh taxation.

The increase of land revenue proper, about £2,000,000 since 1860, is due to the revision of the land settlement which has taken place all over India, except in Bengal, where the well-known permanent settlement of Lord Cornwallis is still maintained. I have dealt with this question in the text.

Apart from the land revenue proper, there are the local cesses, called provincial rates, imposed in 1869–71 and in 1877–78, and now amounting for the whole of India, including Bengal, to about £2,300,000.—*Gazette of India*, March 15, 1879.

There are, besides, the Patwari (village revenue officials) cesses of the North-West Provinces and Madras, amounting to about £475,000 (see note †, p. 11), imposed since 1860.

The salt-tax has been gradually equalised throughout India. On the whole it has been greatly raised during the last 20 years in Southern India and Scinde, while it has been alternately raised and lowered in Northern India and Bengal.

Up to 1850 Madras and Bombay paid ¾ of a rupee per maund (i.e. 82 lbs.), they now pay 2½ rupees. According to latest accounts, the consumption of Government salt during the last few years remains much the same, though it is probably supplemented by illicit supplies.

The North-West Provinces, Oudh, Punjab, and Central Provinces now pay 2½ rupees per maund; a few years ago they paid more. In 1843 the North-

West Provinces paid 2 rupees per maund; the other three provinces were not then British territory. Bengal now pays 2 rupees 14 annas per maund—a little more than the rest. A writer in the *Quarterly Review*, April 1880, seems correct in putting the increase of taxation under this head since 1850 at 1¾ million sterling. In the *Fortnightly* of April 1876, Sir G. Campbell wrote:—'Salt was subjected by the natives to petty duties, like other articles, but in no native state, so far as I am aware, was it ever made the subject of very high duties, and a special source of large revenue, such as it is with us.' He suggested that it should be lowered and income-tax put on. It is now a tax of 2000 per cent. on the prime cost of the article. Each family of five pays about 4*s.* per annum.

The Indian Government has lately made arrangements with native States which possess salt mines, whereby it hires the mines and works them itself. Although compensation has been given, yet some months ago there were rumours in some of the Anglo-Indian papers that the native Governments thought themselves hardly dealt with. Native States now contribute something to the salt-tax. Perhaps this is only fair, as the paramount power practically relieves them of a good deal of military expenditure. The lengthy customs-hedge in Northern India, originally 1,600 miles in length, has been destroyed. The construction of the Rajpatana railway is said to have cheapened salt in Northern India.

The customs tariff has undergone considerable changes during the last ten years, especially in the case of cotton import duties, with the result of a loss to the revenue of about half a million sterling. Part of this, £155,000, was due to the abolition of the inland customs line, whereby duties on sugar were given up. There have been some remissions in export duties.

The excise revenue has increased largely in the last twenty years; but I have not been able to discover what part of this increase is due to heavier taxation; but I believe the excise has been made more severe since 1860.

The stamp revenue has also increased largely during the same period; but part of this increase is said to be due to changes made in the payment of judicial fees. The *Quarterly Review* puts the increase of taxation at half a million sterling since 1850. This part of the revenue ought to be carefully watched, as in a country where the masses are so poor it is difficult to secure justice with heavy fees to pay. If it is to be feared that with lighter fees there would be more litigation, it is obviously not desirable to increase the causes of litigation, as is being done at present by passing new codes. Perhaps it is thought that a new source of supply will be thereby opened up. The appeals against license-tax assessments must have brought in a certain amount of money, as fees ranging from one to eight annas were exacted for each petition.

The changes made in the assessed taxes since 1860 are mentioned in Appendix XI. They now yield £515,000.

Municipal taxation amounts to nearly one and a half millions sterling, the three presidency towns paying about half a million, the 894 district municipalities about one million. This sum is raised partly by octroi, partly by assessed taxes.

In the face of this gradual increase of taxation and of the frequent changes made in connection therewith, even if no fresh taxes have been imposed, it is well to quote the utterances of two Viceroys: 'A feeling of discontent and dissatisfaction,' wrote Lord Mayo in 1872, 'existed among every class both European and native, on account of the constant increase of taxation that had been going on, and the continuance of that feeling was a political danger, the magnitude of which could hardly be over-estimated.' With this remark, Lord Northbrook, when examined before the Committee on Public Works, entirely agreed, adding, 'India is a country in which it is very unwise to be constantly altering taxation; to be constantly imposing fresh taxation.'

APPENDIX III.

According to a speech of Sir J. Strachey published in the *Gazette of India* on March 24, 1877, what is known as the Decentralisation scheme was established in the year 1871–2. Experience had shown that there was a regular scramble by the Local Governments for imperial funds, and that in consequence there was great waste.

Commencing with that year, the financial control of the following services was transferred to the Local Governments: jails, police, education, registration, medical, printing, roads, and civil buildings. They were to be allowed to arrange their own expenditure under each head, and a gross sum, £5,600,000, was made over to them from Imperial revenues. Local cesses were at the same time imposed for local purposes, but the Imperial revenues practically got the benefit of the increase, as these cesses were included in the gross sum assigned, and the Local Governments received less by £400,000 than during the previous year.

In 1877 it was thought advisable to make assignments as to income as well as expenditure. Receipts under stamps, excise, land, and justice, and other miscellaneous heads were handed over to the Local Governments. Thus, the North-West Province had £698,400 made over to it under these heads and £653,600 advanced from Imperial revenues. Any future increase of revenue from stamps, &c. for the ensuing three years was to be divided equally. Arrangements were also made as regards Public Works, and future profits were to be divided. I believe that similar arrangements have been made with the other Local Governments.

In carrying out this extension of the decentralisation scheme, the Indian Government again imposed fresh taxation, originally known as famine insurance taxation, consisting of a license-tax on traders throughout India, and a land-cess in all the provinces, except Bombay and Madras, of 2 per cent on the share of the rental retained by the landowners.

As some doubts were expressed whether the money so raised would be applied to the prevention and relief of famine, Lord Lytton, in a speech delivered December 27, 1877, gave assurances that 'funds locally raised should be locally applied.' He further stated that 'the sole justification of the increased taxation which has just been imposed upon the people of India for the purpose of insuring their empire against the worst calamities of future famine, so far as such an insurance can now be practically provided, is the pledge we have given that a sum not less than a million and a half sterling, which exceeds the amount of the additional contributions obtained from the people for this purpose, shall be annually applied to it. We have pledged ourselves not to spend one rupee of the special resources thus created upon works of a different character.'

In a speech delivered on February 9, 1878, Sir J. Strachey explained to the Legislative Council that 'the object is a perfectly simple one. These new taxes are required for the sole purpose of giving us year by year a sufficient surplus of income over expenditure to meet these famine charges.' He then stated that it was the intention of the Government to raise £15,000,000 in ten years, and either pay off debt or construct famine relief works. He wound up his speech with these words:—'This explanation will show the Council, how either by direct discharge of debt or by the investment of money in productive public works, if the circumstances of the time should render that course most suitable, charges on revenue may be extinguished or new incomes created which shall enable the Government to borrow in the future to the full extent to which the proceeds of the new taxes are applied, and that a true famine insurance fund will thus have been created.' This minute was appended to the budget of 1877-8.

The Viceroy's minute of March 12, 1878, was couched in the same terms. The purposes of the extra taxes were defined as 'direct discharge of debt in times of prosperity, or investments of surplus revenue in productive public works,' further described as 'cheap railroads and extended irrigation works.'

In spite of these repeated assurances, in its retrenchment circular of June 16, 1879, the Indian Government began to speak of 'prevention of debt' as one of the objects of these taxes. This is a very *general* object for taxation, and can hardly explain the fact that these taxes are only imposed on *special* classes, i.e., traders and land-owners.

It may be urged that when money was required for war, it would have been absurd not to make use of the fresh taxes. But in that case the Government ought to have made a frank confession that its scheme was impracticable, and have asked leave to divert to general purposes the money raised for a special object. It ought also to have imposed an income-tax on salaried and professional classes, previously exempted on the ground that they were not affected by famine. It ought anyhow not to have thrown away over £200,000 by partial repeal of the cotton duties.

Instead of any part of the funds raised being locally applied, the Local Governments have had to contribute the sum of £670,000 during the past and current year, while the repairs of works have had to be stopped.

It is obvious, therefore, that the decentralisation scheme has hitherto been the means not of encouraging local prudence and thrift, but of enabling the Imperial revenues to be gradually increased at the expense of the Local Governments. The result is that the latter are beginning to see whether they cannot shift some of their burdens, hitherto borne by provincial funds, on municipal and other local funds. A Calcutta paper lately pointed out that the Bengal Government was trying to force some municipal bodies to pay more towards roads in spite of the fact that a special road-cess had been imposed on the province a few years ago.

We shall probably hear of further 'changes in the form of accounts,' too often a euphemistic phrase for fresh taxation. Funds will be raised in non-regulation provinces for the payment of revenue officials hitherto supported in less burdensome ways by the landowners. It is this insidious method of increasing taxation that requires careful watching.

A provincial budget has generally four heads of income: (1) Imperial; (2) Provincial, i.e. the money may be spent anyhow; (3) Incorporated Local with primary lien, i.e. revenue officials and village watchmen funds, and the like; (4) appropriated trust funds for local purposes.

The tendency, under pressure from the Imperial Government, will be* to turn (3) into (2), and (4) into (3). When that is done the various local funds will have to be replenished by more house taxes and assessed taxes.

Municipal accounts are kept separately, but if the outlay on roads for which they are now responsible were to be increased, or city endowments were to be diverted,† vexatious direct taxes would have to be imposed, especially if Sir J. Strachey's Bill to restrict, in some cases practically to abolish, octroi were to be carried. The

* In the Administration Report of the North-Western Provinces and Oudh for 1877–8, I read, 'It is the declared policy of the Supreme Government to reduce these funds (i.e., incorporated local) to such a minimum as is consistent with the equitable administration of them, and under recent instructions several have been, or shortly will be, removed from the appropriated list, and incorporated with provincial accounts, such as the various Record funds, Tarai improvement, Oudh school fund.' The Report of 1878–9 states that this has been carried out by order from Government. This means that funds raised for special purposes are to be used for general purposes, if there is a surplus.

† I heard of one flagrant attempt of this sort, but I am not at liberty to give the facts.

Quarterly Review of April 1880 says, that 'the Bengal road-cess has been a great success,' and 'perhaps if we availed ourselves more largely of local institutions, and proceeded from below upwards, developing village institutions, and gradually coming to those higher in the scale, we might succeed better than we do.'

Experience proves that such a development merely means putting on the screw of taxation, and if, as I have shown, the imposition of local cesses results in the Local Governments having less and less to spend, while they try to squeeze out more and more, we may find centres of discontent springing up in those very local bodies which it is our boast to have called into life. The decentralisation scheme wants a thorough investigation, if it is not to be a mere farce, not to say the cause of grave political danger.

It is impossible to doubt that Local Governments have been more careful in expenditure since 1870, but if the Imperial Government from time to time demands a readjustment of accounts, all the advantage of this well-intended reform disappears. Mr. Hunter says that 'Lord Mayo distinctly announced his determination that the demands on the people for provincial purposes should not be indefinitely or too rapidly increased.' 'The natives of India,' he adds, 'draw as yet but little distinction between municipal, provincial, and Imperial taxation. All are equally attributed to the British Government, and all are equally disliked. Indeed some experienced administrators believe that a tax becomes the more obnoxious in India as the power from which it emanates is nearer and more familiar.'

If district officers assume more and more the position of tax-gatherers and tax-projectors, it is quite clear that their personal influence will soon disappear. They will be regarded as the fleecers rather than the fathers of their districts, and every native will avoid their presence. As worked out by men like Sir J. Strachey, Lord Mayo's scheme may become an incarnate curse.

The Famine Commission proposes special local rates in order to provide further famine funds. What guarantee is there that these fresh funds would not be 'diverted' or 'temporarily suspended,' as the phrase goes? It also suggests that the famine insurance cess should now be extended to Bombay and Madras, which have hitherto been exempted on account of the recent famine. No doubt this will help to replenish the cash balances, but it will deplete the ryots' stores of grain.

APPENDIX IV.

It is very interesting and instructive to compare the state of Mysore (1) under native rule; (2) under European supervision; (3) under bureaucratic routine. I cannot do better than reprint an article which appeared in the *Pioneer* of July 22, 1879, on the administration of Mysore :—

During the present century Mysore has been the scene of more administrative changes than any other part of India; in fact, it seems to have been the 'body vile' on which all sorts of political experiments were tried. From 1799 to 1811 the province was administered with great success by the renowned Brahmin, Pirnia, in the name of the young Rajah. He was assisted by three English officials, and by their joint efforts the prosperity of the country was greatly enhanced, and a surplus of two crores of rupees was accumulated in the treasury. In 1811 the young Rajah, having attained his sixteenth year, dismissed the faithful Pirnia, and assumed the reins of Government. By his utter disregard for truth and entire subservience to the influence of favourites he threw the country into great disorder. In consequence of the unfavourable reports of the Resident, he was warned by Sir T. Monro, Governor of Madras, that if the reform of the administration was not commenced forthwith, the direct interference of the British Government would be unavoidable. The effect of this warning was very short-lived, and in 1832 Lord Bentinck, with the approval of the Court of Directors, transferred the entire administration into the hands of British officers, consigning the Rajah to the state of a pensioner. For twenty-five years Sir Mark Cubbon ruled the country with such signal success that he called forth the strongest expressions of praise from Lord Dalhousie. 'Every department had felt the hand of reform. In that of civil and criminal justice, regularity, order, and purity had been introduced, where under native rule caprice, uncertainty, and corruption prevailed. Taxes had been reduced to the extent of eleven lakhs of rupees a year, and the revenue had nevertheless increased from forty-four to eighty-two lakhs.' A recent return made to the House of Commons, shows that in the year 1864 there was to be found in the Mysore treasuries an accumulated surplus of about 102 lakhs of rupees. The principle of Sir M. Cubbon's administration was the employment of a native staff carefully supervised by four Europeans at a cost for the European agency of £13,000 a year. The native system of revenue assessment, of keeping the public accounts, was retained, but simple rules were from time to time issued for the administration of justice. Small works of irrigation, suited to the wants of the people, were encouraged, and were carried out by the natives themselves. Though the province suffered from time to time owing to the want of rain, yet it always managed to tide over the bad harvests without any disaster. On various occasions the Rajah applied for the restoration of the Government into his own hands, but his request was refused by five successive Viceroys, on the ground that there would be no security against the return of the previous misrule; and it was distinctly proved by a careful investigation of all the original papers of Lord Wellesley, that the treaty of 1799 was personal and not dynastic. Soon after the retirement of Sir M. Cubbon a great change was made in the principle of administration. Under the influence of the

Dalhousian zeal for progress, the European agency was gradually increased, entailing an expenditure of £90,000 instead of £13,000; a public works department was established; the opinions of the civilian staff, the requirements of the country, and the needs of the people were ruthlessly set aside; larger salaries had to be granted, and the surplus gradually disappeared. In 1863 the Bombay settlement officer appeared on the scene. The assessment appears to have been light, but, in spite of that fact, 'the ownership of the land,' according to Mr. Elliott's Famine Report, 'is fast passing out of the hands of those who are directly interested in it.' The ryot is rapidly becoming a metayer tenant-at-will. The enclosure of the forests and the putting up of waste lands to auction must have made a considerable difference to the peasant in the rearing of cattle. Moreover, the influence of the village system, according to the same report, has been very much undermined by the rigorous red-tapism of the settlement officer; his imperiousness has frightened away the *patel* or headman, 'who used to be the father of his village, the connecting link to prevent the disintegration of the ryotwari system and the dispersion of the ryots; the man to whom the ryot looks for a loan, if he is unable to pay his revenue, and the labourer for an advance of food, if employment is slack and his stock has run out.' If we couple such changes with the fact that the rainfall is very variable, and the revenue, however lightly assessed, is exacted with great punctuality, it seems doubtful whether the Bombay settlement has been altogether a boon to the country, in spite of the thirty years' leases which have been granted. Happily for the province, the process of further Europeanisation has been stopped. As far as the official agency and the Public Works Department are concerned, a return is to be made to the system of administration carried on by Sir Mark Cubbon. Europeans will only be retained for the higher judicial and executive work. The Forest Department, whose independence caused so much difficulty in the late famine, is to be abolished and to be absorbed into the districts, and the three specially trained European conservators in charge of the three western districts will be placed under the district officers. The Public Works Department is also to be cut down. There will be a large saving of expenditure effected under these different heads, and the province will have some chance of recovering from the effects of its terrible famine.

In 1880 the young Maharajah will have the Government

of Mysore entrusted to him, subject to such conditions as may be determined at the time. It appears from a recent notification that he will be advised by a council, but we are not informed as to the exact nature of its composition. It is, however, obvious that the Indian Government does not intend to place Mysore under an entirely native administration watched over by a Resident. The young Prince is to be kept in European leading-strings of a substantial kind. We hope that the various officers who have taken part in his dry-nursing may have produced a ruler worthy of their solicitous attentions. To place a prince who has been made the subject of so many experiments over a province which has been similarly treated, would clearly be the height of rashness, unless some strong safeguards are provided. It is difficult to feel very confident about the success of the system which is to be shortly introduced, but a good opportunity is offered to the Indian Government of trying on a small scale how far a native agency can be made efficient under European supervision. It would appear that the principle of administration which has been working for the last twenty years has proved somewhat useless, if it has not seriously injured the future prospects of the province. The old staff of native officials has been roughly set aside, and their successors do not appear equal to the task. 'The old class of amildars,' says Mr. Elliott, 'were uneducated, but men of strong will, common sense, and much intelligence, who knew how to govern and make themselves obeyed. It is a general complaint that the new men who pass from a school education and a university degree to a clerk's post in a Bangalore office, and thence to the office of amildar, are found wanting in practical knowledge and governing power; and it is a phrase indicating bitter scorn in Mysore to call a man a B.A.' The future council will do well to seek some of the old specimens, if they have not been improved off the face of the country by the pretentious young men who are described by Mr. Saunders 'as having little respect for the authority of anyone from the Secretary of State downwards,' and who, in spite of 'the glitter of their tinsel accomplishments,' are regarded with distrust by the more experienced officials. This may merely be due to the natural prejudice felt by staid seniors against the young idea, but the enthusiastic reformer is apt to forget that human nature, especially in the East, is very conservative, and objects to being governed by *novi homines*, however brilliant their brains may be.'

The following further remarks on the recently introduced land revenue settlement appeared in the *Pioneer Mail* of July 1, 1880:—

The revenue settlement of the province is being made on the same system which has been tried and failed in Bombay. Judging by some facts buried away in the body of the report and unnoticed in the summary, this system appears unsuited for Mysore. In the surveyed taluks over 106,000 acres net—i.e. after deducting lands newly taken up from the quantity relinquished—were relinquished as against 30,000 acres in the unsurveyed taluks. No explanation is offered as to why, in those taluks where the revenue system is supposed to be perfect, more than three times the net quantity of land has been thrown up as compared with that in those taluks where the old system is still in force. Again, the area of land rented out under a tenure of a division of crop between the Government and the cultivator was considerably increased. This was avowedly done in order to promote the cultivation of abandoned lands which were rented out on terms unusually favourable to the cultivator. The result of this was that, although this tenure is directly opposed in principle to the system we are introducing, more land was taken up, and more money was obtained per acre from the land. The wet land let on the division of crops tenure brought in Rs. 6-3 per acre, while the new wet land taken upon the Bombay system of assessment was not only less in quantity, but only gave Rs. ·96 per acre, less than one rupee per acre. These figures show a very serious state of affairs. Putting aside the direct loss to the State—a loss it can ill afford after the late famine—the figures of increased area cultivated prove that the tenure of a division of crops is more suited to the genius of the Mysore people than the system we are now forcing upon them. Is it wise to continue a rigid system of assessment which is pecuniarily bad for the State and prejudicial to the interests of its people? Not one-half the number of taluks have yet been settled, and, judging by the past rate of working, it will take fifteen years more before the province is completed.

No better instance than that of Mysore could be found to exhibit the disastrous results of a large and highly paid European staff, carrying out with ruthless energy its so-called administrative and economical improvements, irrespective of the price to be paid for them. Mr. B. Elliot, 'the Mysore planter,' in a book published some time ago, went so far as to prophesy a famine if the resources of the country are drained for extravagant public works. His prophecy has been fulfilled. It appears from the Famine Report that Mysore had many a time been on the verge of famine, but the stores of grain had staved it off. The recent catastrophe seems to have been in a large measure due to the exhaustion of resources which, as I have pointed out in the text, is admitted in the official report. This fact is very much slurred over in the Famine Commission's Blue Book.

It may not be possible just at present to cut down the number of Europeans in the British Provinces, but a few well-paid officers, with more independence of action and more freedom from office work, would, no doubt, with the aid of native subordinates, lessen the cost of administration.

It is usually said that, although natives are good for judicial work, they are not fitted for executive. But it must be remembered that as pleaders and petty judges they have been able to get more experience in the first line than in the second. They would certainly require to be men of influence and position, as Lord Lytton lately pointed out, not merely Calcutta B.A.'s, but if they were placed under good supervision, there seems no reason to suppose that they would not do excellent work.

According to some figures given me by a friend, there are in the North-West Provinces and Oudh 857 Europeans altogether, drawing 577,471 rupees a month, their salaries ranging from 3,750 to 50 rupees, while there are 853 natives, altogether drawing 165,880 rupees a month, their salaries ranging from 800 to 50 rupees. All the natives drawing lower pay are omitted: they form a large number. Although it could not be expected that Englishmen would serve under natives, yet, as Col. Chesney recently suggested in the *Fortnightly*, there is still plenty of room for natives in the lower grades of the service. It would obviously be very unfair to Englishmen, who have had certain prospects held out to them, to find natives promoted or brought in over their heads, as was recently the case with a judicial appointment in Oudh under pressure from Lord Lytton. It is not advisable to irritate a whole service, on whose willing work everything depends.

It may not be wholly irrelevant to add my testimony to that of Professor Monier Williams to one of India's great dangers, namely, over-centralisation. I have pointed out in another appendix what a complete delusion the decentralisation scheme has hitherto proved, but, even if that scheme were made a reality, it is as well to recognise that its principle, at least in administrative matters, requires to be still further extended.

An Indian province is a very wide world; that of the North-West Provinces and Oudh covers more than 100,000 square miles, with a population of over 40 millions, and all its varied needs are not necessarily measured by the minds of a few secretaries. However powerful their calibre may be, their experience may be small, and yet they are continually justifying their position by worrying the lives of district officers with their pertinacious obtrusiveness. 'Half the time of a collector,' writes Professor Monier Williams with literal truth, 'is now occupied in replying to the inquiries of inquisitive under-secretaries. Every post brings piles of official documents and demands for reports and written statistics on every conceivable subject, while, in return, piles of foolscap find their way from the collector's cutchery into the pigeon-holes of the under-secretary's office. There the precious bundles of foolscap are forthwith entombed, and from these graves there is seldom any resurrection to the light of day.' The best way to get rid of all this writing would be to exact a heavy fine from each secretary who spent over a certain sum on stationery, &c. The amount of waste in administration reports is frightful. They bristle with fatuous figures. The last North-West Province and Oudh Administration Report has 500 pages of all conceivable statistics. In fact, the Indian Government is rapidly becoming a paper despotism, with a Press-Commissioner as the presiding genius, working through the medium of the post and telegraph. He is the last sweet baby of the bureaucracy, and his babblings are so sacred that criticism is regarded as blasphemous.

APPENDIX V.

The returns for State Irrigation Works presented to the Parliamentary Committee on Public Works are as follows :—

	Capital Expenditure	Receipts	Working Expenses	Interest
	£	£	£	£
Bengal	4,072,742	23,043	52,949	182,237
North-Western Province	4,939,527	375,659	145,015	222,279
Punjab	3,335,503	288,360	136,214	150,097
Scinde	667,938	161,368	—	30,047
Bombay	665,938	6,090	—	29,967
Madras	1,881,241	376,473	62,572	84,656
	15,562,655	1,228,993	396,750	700,319

According to these figures there is an excess revenue over and above the working expenses of £131,924.* But from this, as the Committee points out, must be deducted £46,453 for the Madras Irrigation Company's works, which were bought up by the State.

Moreover, it is admitted that the returns are incomplete, that there is no allowance for old native works, that the separation of the accounts for irrigation works from those of ordinary public works has only been effected very recently, and that a share in the total cost (£2,369,999) of establishments and furlough allowances in the Public Works Department has not been assigned. Anyone who takes the trouble to examine the back budgets in the *Gazettes of India* will find great reason for doubting whether the cost of repairs in the past has been included, and whether the capital expenditure is not greater than that given above; certainly the interest on capital outlay, before the works paid at all, has been left out of the account. The above figures, therefore, which, at first sight, appear very favourable, cannot be taken as wholly reliable.

A closer examination of the returns shows great variety in the results obtained; while some works, such as those on the Cauvery (a restored native work), the Godavery, and Krishna in the Madras Presidency, and the Jumna Canals, in Northern India, have been very remunerative, there are others, like the Bengal Canals, that have only paid a little more than their working expenses.

On the other hand, it must not be forgotten that, apart from their direct returns in the shape of water rates

* The returns this year are better by transfer of land revenue attributed to irrigation works.

and increased land revenue, they have preserved an enormous area of crops in years of drought. In the famine of 1860–61 the West Jumna Canal is calculated to have preserved half a million acres, and in the famine of 1877–8 the Ganges Canal performed yeoman service.

Moreover, the capital laid out on canal construction, unlike that laid out on railways, has been to a great extent spent in the country, and its benefits are much more appreciated by the natives; and if their engineering talent, of which the most experienced Anglo-Indian engineers have spoken in the highest terms, were to be further utilised, the, at present, heavy establishment charges might be greatly curtailed.

Lord Lytton's best work has been the initiation of retrenchment under this head, but the axe has still to be laid at the root of the tree—Cooper's Hill College—which was, in 1874, declared by Lieut.-Col. Tyrrell, an officer of fifteen years' experience as an executive engineer in various parts of India, to be 'a disgraceful imposition on India.'

Mr. Sowerby, who was examined before the Committee on Public Works, and who has had a large amount of experience in India as an engineer, said, 'The natives of India have a better knowledge of the application of water for purposes of irrigation than gentlemen or engineers sent out from this country. Irrigation is, as it were, indigenous to the country.'

According to the candid admission of Sir A. Cotton and others, the most successful English irrigation works have been those that have been carried out on native lines. What the Indian Government appears to have lost sight of is the different requirements of different parts of India. The battle of productive works has been waged by the advocates of railways and canals, while sufficient attention has not been paid to other methods of irrigation, familiar to natives and not requiring any scientific knowledge or costly establishments.

A vast continent like India necessarily varies in its physical conditions. Canals may suit one part, tanks another, wells another. According to the best authorities there are hundreds of tanks in Southern India out of repair, while in the North-West Provinces and Oudh a well-system is considered by district officers to be most suitable. The teaching of centuries has not been so utterly lost on the native mind that engineers, primed with Western science but wanting in Eastern experience, must be imported to irrigate the country. Instead of killing native intelligence and thwarting the play of self-interest the Government ought to give every kind of encouragement by offering careers in its service and helping private individuals in protecting their lands against drought. Settlement regulations seem at present to have the very opposite tendency.

No one can doubt that water is India's great necessity; railways are at most a luxury. The produce of the land must be increased before improved communications are required to circulate it.

The Famine Commissioners calculate the annual surplus yield at five million tons of food, but Messrs. Caird and Sullivan say that they are unable to place confidence in this estimate. 'The average annual export of rice and grain from all India,' the two latter write, 'is one million tons, which should thus leave four million tons to be laid by, a quantity sufficient to feed twenty-four millions of people; as famine comes but once in twelve years, there should in that period be an accumulation surplus sufficient to feed nearly 300 millions; and yet when famine does come, and then affecting at its worst not more than a tenth of that number, it is only by immense pressure on other parts of India, and at a quadrupled price, that the barest sufficiency of supplies can be obtained. This seems clear proof that the alleged surplus must be greatly overestimated. . . . . Population is increasing, the price of food is rising, the production of it, as shown by exports, scarcely advances, whilst, as the number of the landless class who depend on wages is constantly growing, the supply of labour in the absence of industries other than agriculture must soon exceed the demand. . . . . The food of two-thirds of the people of India is grain, and of one-third rice. The annual surplus of rice, as shown by the export, is so great that a sufficient supply from the current crop can be always relied on to meet a partial rice famine. But the export of food grain, other than rice, from India, during each of the last ten years, has been less than one day's consumption of the grain-eating population. There would thus appear to be no sufficient annual surplus within the country to meet the demand of a severe grain famine, without drawing part of their ordinary food from the unaffected districts, thereby diminishing their supply, raising the price, and thus extending the area and general pressure of the famine. This has been the uniform effect of drawing supplies suddenly to the famine districts from other parts of India.'

The question is, How is money to be got for those larger works which Government alone can undertake, and which may not prove directly remunerative? The Famine Commissioners propose special local rates for protective works, and there seems no reason to doubt that if money so raised were to be locally expended, as was originally proposed under the Famine Insurance Scheme, there would be less objection to such rates. But some distinct safeguards ought to be established against their misappropriation. The breach of faith, of which the Government has lately been guilty, has largely contributed towards discouraging the efforts of the Local Governments in protecting the land from drought. A trust fund, managed by a provincial body, largely composed of district officers and native gentlemen, might secure the proper application of famine insurance taxes.

APPENDIX VI.

'It (Political Economy) has often been put forward, not as a theory of the principal causes affecting wealth in *certain* societies, but as the theory of the principal, sometimes even of all, the causes affecting wealth in *every* society; and this has occasioned many and strong doubts about it. Travellers fresh from the sight, and historians fresh from the study of peculiar and various states of society, look with dislike and disbelief on a single set of abstract propositions which claim, as they think, to be applicable to all such societies, and to explain a most important part of most of them. I cannot here pause to say how far particular English economists have justified this accusation; I only say that, taking the whole body of them, there is much ground for it, and that in almost every one of them there is some ground. No doubt almost every one—every one of importance—has admitted that there is a 'friction' in society which counteracts the effects of the causes treated of. But in general they leave their readers with the idea that, after all, this friction is but subordinate; that probably in the course of years it may be neglected; and, at any rate, that the causes assigned in the science of Political Economy, as they treat it, are the main and principal ones. Now, I hold that these causes are only the main ones in a single kind of society—a society of grown-up competitive commerce, such as we have in England; that it is only in such societies that the other and counteracting forces can be set together under the minor head of 'friction'; but that in other societies these other causes—in some cases one, and in some another—are the most effective ones, and that the greatest confusion arises if you try to fit on *un*economical societies the theories only true of, and only proved as to, economical ones. In my judgment, we need—not that the authority of our Political Economy should be impugned, but that it should be *minimised*; that we should realise distinctly where it is established and where not; that its sovereignty should be upheld, but its frontiers marked. And until this is done I am sure that there will remain the same doubt and hesitation in many minds about the science that there is now.'—'Economic Studies,' p. 16–17.

The easy transferability of labour and capital is pointed out, as underlying the reasonings of English economists. This condition is not present in all countries.

According to the Bluebook on Moral and Material Progress of India, for 1878–79, there are 30,000 natives working in the Bombay mills. There may be 10,000 more in other parts of India. There are also 134,000 working on the railways.

The above report says that year by year a large

number of cotton weavers is thrown on the land. The Indian Famine Commissioners write as follows (par. 103): 'A main cause of the disastrous consequences of Indian famines, and one of the greatest difficulties in the way of providing relief in an effectual shape, is to be found in the fact that the great mass of the population directly depends on agriculture, and there is no other industry from which any considerable part of the community derives its support. The failure of the usual rain thus deprives the labouring class, as a whole, not only of the ordinary supplies of food obtainable at prices within their reach, but also of the sole employment by which they can earn the means of procuring it. The complete remedy for this condition of things will be found only in the development of industries other than agriculture, and independent of the fluctuations of the seasons. With a population so dense as that of India, these considerations are of the greatest weight, and they are rendered still more serious by the fact that numbers who have no other employment than agriculture, are in large parts of the country greatly in excess of what is really required for the thorough cultivation of the land. So far as this is the case the result must be, that the part of the population which is in excess of the requirements of agriculture eats up the profits that would otherwise spring from the industry of the community. How many thousands of native weavers have been thrown on the land by Lancashire competition it is difficult to say; but there is no doubt that their number is yearly increasing, and the community has to support them in time of famine in return for cheaper cotton goods. Is this economy? If the natives were willing to migrate or emigrate, then free trade would be beneficial, but it has been thrust on the country irrespective of native ways, and of the difficulty of starting new industries. A dull monotony, varied by periodical famines, is becoming more and more the chief feature of India's economic life.' Our administration presupposes an ever-active intelligence, while we are destroying that variety of industry which nourishes it.

APPENDIX VII.

According to the last report on Indian railways the capital spent on guaranteed lines up to March 1879 is £96,725,679, and that on state lines up to October 1878 is £21,291,076. Of the former £43,874,346 have been withdrawn in England, £51,556,517 in India; of the latter £5,227,132 in England, and £16,063,944 in India. The gross receipts of the guaranteed railways during the last year were £9,503,721, their working expenses £4,501,693, and interest on capital, raised for the most part at 5 per cent., £4,708,134. There remained as surplus profits £293,894 to be divided between the State and the Companies.

Only three railways, the East Indian, the Great Indian Peninsula, and the Eastern Bengal, paid over their 5 per cent. interest; but their excess returns made up the deficiencies of the rest, so that now for two consecutive years the state has not had to pay any interest out of its ordinary revenues. But it must be remembered that war has aided the railways during the last year, as famine did in the previous one. The interest advanced by the State up to 1878 reached the enormous sum of £26,586,039. If this is added to the capital originally borrowed, and 4½ per cent. is charged on it, there still remains an annual deficit of nearly one million sterling. The state railways, commenced in 1869, the capital for which has been raised at 4¼ per cent., have never yet paid their interest. Their gross receipts are £901,032, working expenses £705,245, and net receipts £195,787,* to meet interest of between £800,000 and £900,000. The loss in interest up to 1878 was £2,221,343. Some of these railways are not yet completed, and it is hoped that they will in the future pay better; but at present they are very far from being a commercial success. It must, moreover, be pointed out that as the capital for guaranteed and state railways has for the most part been raised in gold, and the state has to pay in silver, when the rate of exchange is as low as it was a year ago, i.e. a rupee = 1*s.* 7¾*d.*, there is a loss of about 1 million sterling on the remittances for interest. In the present uncertainty of the silver market it is as well to remember this fact, which materially affects the success of railways.

A careful examination of the whole railway system of India shows that although the earliest lines are beginning to pay, yet the later ones are likely to be a heavy burden on the state for some time to come, if not for an indefinite period. The trade of the country does not give any signs of such a large expansion as would justify any further extension of the railway system. Since 1860 the trade of India has hardly doubled, while the miles of railway have increased from 626 to about 8,500. Although the passenger traffic is steadily in-

* This deficiency is this year nearly met by increased receipts from railways on account of war and purchase of East Indian Railway, but the latter entails outlay of £630,000.

creasing, thirty-eight and a half millions being conveyed in 1878, the goods traffic is uncertain from year to year.

The chairman of the Bengal Chamber of Commerce, in his address on the half-yearly report in last June, said: 'Notwithstanding the opening up of the country by light railways and roads, and the increased facilities for bringing produce to market, I do not see in what particular direction we can look for any great increase to our exports; opium, rice, cotton, indigo, and jute seem to me to have attained their highest limit. Tea has decreased in total value and seeds cannot be relied on. Wheat, it was thought at one time, might become a large factor in the case; but I am afraid India cannot now compete with America in this article. Altogether the item in the budget of loss by exchange will, I fear, always be a serious one, and unless some strenuous effort is made to lessen the amount of the Secretary of State's drawings, it may well be that it will land the country eventually in a state of hopeless bankruptcy.' With such a prospect it would appear prudent to discontinue building any more railways, except perhaps those of a very light nature, for which local loans might be raised.

Of course it may be said that for strategical and famine purposes railways are invaluable. No one can deny the use of the four main lines, the East Indian, the Great Indian Peninsula, the Scinde, Punjab, and Delhi, and the Indus Valley, for the conveyance of troops and stores; but they seem quite sufficient for this object. And as regards the use of railways in times of famine, it must not be forgotten that they have had to be paid for out of taxation which has drained the country's resources, and that by the opening of markets the growth of non-edible crops has been encouraged and the amount of grain produce has become less. In a time of dearth the railways may bring food; but the State gives the money. The question arises how far the latter has first helped to deplete the local stores, and whether the custom of storing grain in a country which is periodically visited by drought, is not on the whole the most economical way of providing against famine. Railways have equalised prices throughout India, but it is by levelling them up. The great rise in 20 years is chiefly due to the influx of silver for construction of railways. The logical result of our economic principles as applied to India is the starvation of the agricultural labourer and artisan. He finds prices rising out of proportion to his wages, which are kept down by excessive competition. It is absolutely ruinous for the State to spend £15,000,000 every ten years on famine relief, and yet this is what railways are bringing about under the pressure of public opinion in England. It would certainly seem cheaper for the Indian Government to begin at the other end, not the relief but the prevention of famine, and to pay a little more attention to what is done in the best-governed native states, as regards land revenue matters, the prevention of the indebtedness of the agriculturist, and the encouragement of well-building, &c. Less heroic and expensive methods are required. More ought to be done by the people and less for them, if we are not to demoralise the whole country. Prudential checks on population are discouraged by a haphazard revenue system.

APPENDIX VIII.

The Deccan Ryots Relief Bill, according to the summary given by Mr. Hope, secures—

(1) Precautions against fraud.

(2) The interposition of friendly conciliation between disputants previous to litigation.

(3) The approximation of courts to homes of the people.

(4) Simplification of procedure and diminution of expenses and technicalities.

(5) Equitable jurisdiction.

(6) Finality of judicial decisions.

(7) Prompt enforcement of decrees.

(8) Discharge of the debtor.

As cheap and easy justice has often been put forward as one of the advantages of English rule, it is well to listen to the opinion of the Deccan Riots Commission on this point :—'There is another cause which requires mention here as tending to make the action of the courts oppressive to debtors, namely, the high costs of suits. The costs of suits fall upon the debtors, and so long as they do not exceed the actual cost of the litigation of which the debtors are the cause, the charge is fair. But the income from the 88 subordinate courts last year was Rs. 16.89.744 ; while the expenditure on the courts, including the salaries of judges and all officers attached to the courts, was only Rs. 6.90.717. These courts thus yielded a net revenue of nearly ten lakhs of rupees. It is impossible to ascertain precisely how much of this surplus is absorbed in the support of the Appellate Courts. But we need not say that the object of courts is not to yield a revenue, and it is plainly proper that any surplus that may be derived from them should be devoted to improving the administration of justice in them, and not to any other object. There appears reason to think that some of the miscellaneous court charges—such as fees for copying, costs in execution and attachment processes and the like—are unduly burdensome, and if this is the case they should be reduced.'

The Bombay High Court must have a very easy time, considering the number of its judges. The Punjab, with a population of seventeen millions, has only a Judicial Commissioner to constitute a High Court of Appeal; Bombay, with sixteen millions, has eight judges. Allowance being made for Bombay itself, it is difficult to see how there can be work for so many. As a fact, I found on inquiry at the court that off-days are very numerous. The Calcutta High Court has only eleven judges, and yet the population of Bengal and Assam is between sixty and seventy millions. Now that the Deccan Ryots Relief Bill has cut down some of the appellate work, there is still more reason for retrenchment in the outlay on the High Court.

APPENDIX IX.

'Speaking very broadly, it may be said that we found in Hindu law two leading principles, by no means easy to reconcile, but which the Hindus seem in practice to have reconciled : one, family or hereditary responsibility for debt; the other, the inalienability of family property, especially of land; in other words (again speaking broadly, for of course the Hindu law of inheritance and the English law of entail have nothing but a result in common); a general law of entail. Our courts—not apt at reconciling opposed principles, and guided by English notions of justice—have in effect fully carried out the first of these principles and have superseded the second, and Hindu estates in land are therefore exposed to the dangers of the one and have lost the safeguard of the other.

'It may, of course, be said that this result was to be desired; that in England it has now been decided that the freest possible transfer of land is beneficial. But India is not England. In England a constant interchange of classes is going on. Partly from the love of the country, and of rural pursuits, which seems to be innate in the people; partly from the social consideration and political influence which the ownership of land gives; the ambition of the successful man of business is to found and to reside on an estate, and his energy, wealth, and intelligence often make him a better landlord than the man from whom he acquires it; while there are many trades and professions to which the family of the ruined landowner can betake themselves for support, and with fair prospects of success. In India it is not so. The landowner who has lost his estate sinks into abject poverty, embittered by the memory of the position he has lost, and, if a man of energy or influence, becomes politically dangerous. We know what discontent transfer of the rights of landowners to their tenants caused in Hindustan; how much greater is discontent likely to be where the change of ownership injures instead of benefiting the cultivator? The money-lender, on the other hand, who acquires the estate, though he likes the possession of land well enough, has no idea beyond that of getting all he can out of it, and would shrink with horror from the notion of leaving the town life, the society of his caste-fellows, the business habits, and the round of petty gains to which he is accustomed in order to reside in solitary dignity in a remote village. Money-grubbing is the life of these people; to drive sharp bargains is their pleasure and glory; public opinion—except that of their own class, which is that to make money any how is creditable and that the mode in which it is made is amply atoned for by some act of showy liberality—has no influence over them; and they treat their tenants without scruple or remorse as they treat their debtors, as persons whom Providence and the *Sarkar* have delivered into their hands.

'As regards the peasant proprietors of Bombay, there are other noteworthy considerations.

'Speaking generally, when British rule succeeded to that of the Mahrattas in the Bombay Presidency, the land was the property of the State; the cultivators were tenants of Government, and very generally tenants-at-will. The British Government has deliberately divested itself of the ownership of the soil, and has transferred it to its tenants, in order to raise the status of the great and important cultivating class; to improve by the 'magic of property' the wretched Indian husbandry; to confer on the country generally the advantages which economists believe to attend the system of peasant proprietorship.* It is surely intolerable that this measure—one, I believe, of the wisest and most successful ever carried out by an Indian Government—should be rendered nugatory by the diversion to another class, totally unconnected with the

* The Bombay ryot with an erratic land-tax is not at all a peasant proprietor. A permanent settlement *made with the cultivators* has yet to be tried in India.

soil, of the gift which Government made to the cultivators, and that the latter, instead of being, as they were meant to be, owners of their holding, subject to a moderate and fixed assessment, or, as they were, tenants of a Government who at least endeavoured to act towards them with justice and liberality, should become cottier tenants-at-will, or something lower, of hard and grasping landlords.

'For it cannot be too clearly understood that only in the dream of a visionary will the English agricultural system of large landlords, capitalists, farmers of large farms, and peasant labourers for wage, ever be substituted for the *petite culture* of India. Happen what will, each ryot will till his petty holding, but he may be, as we have made him in Bombay, its proprietor; he may be, as in the North-West, a member of a proprietary cultivating community; he may be, as in Rajputana, the customary tenant of an hereditary lord; or he may be, as I fear he is becoming, the predial serf of a money-lender. That the operations of the civil courts are now assisting this result may be judged of by the fact that there were in 1872 over 18,000 sales of immoveable property (lands and houses) in execution of decrees in the Regulation Districts of Bombay against less than 6,000 of moveable property.'

Quoted by the Deccan Commission from a pamphlet by Mr. Pedder, late of the Bombay Civil Service, and now Secretary of the Revenue Department in the India Office.

APPENDIX X.

During Sir H. Maine's tenure of office (1862–69) the chief Bills were those relating to 'Works of Public Utility by Private Companies, Articles of War (native), Breaches of Trust, a number of Bills for the control of High Courts in the Presidency and other towns, Municipal Assessment, the Law of Divorce, Treaties, Imprisonment of Convicts, Civil Justice in various parts, Stamp Duties, Oudh Claims, Bank Receipts, Bill relating to Foreigners, Coolie Emigration, French Bank Bill, Tolls and Port Dues; Customs, a Whipping Bill, Official Trustees, Military Cantonments, Municipal Bills, Small Cause Courts, Magistrates' Courts, Registration of Assurances, Remarriage of Native Converts, Oaths of Justice, &c., Akbar Acts, Civil Procedure, Criminal Jurisdiction, Civil Code, Ceded Lands, &c., Government Forests, Administration of Estates, the Succession and Inheritance of Parsees, Partnership, Indian Companies, Pleaders' Bill, Summary Proceedings on Bills of Exchange, Recorders' Bill, on the Manufacture and Sale of Arms, Assam Tea Company, Execution of Process, Religious Endowments, Mortgagees and Trustees' Property, Removal of Prisoners, Horse-racing, Public Gambling, Escaped Convicts, Presidency Gaols, Murderous Outrages, Madras Salt, Oudh Rent, European Vagrancy, Contagious Diseases, Principal Sudr Amins and Munsifs (Judges), Oudh Talookdars, Native Marriages not Christian, Punjab Tenancy, Lock Hospitals, and others.' This list I have taken from Mr. J. Routledge's *English Rule and Native Opinion in India*.

Some of these Bills, especially those relating to

divorce and marriage, excited great alarm in the native mind.

Sir James Stephen's (1869–1872) chief measures were the Amended Penal Code, the Limitation Act, the Evidence Act, the Contract Act, the Criminal Procedure Code, Acts relating to the Civil Courts of Bengal, Oudh, and Burmah, the Punjab Code, the Punjab Drainage and Canal Act, the Land Acquisition Act, the Hindoo Wills Act, the Native Marriage Act, besides the consolidation of many previously existing Regulations, and various political Acts, such as those for Local cesses and Income Tax. This list is taken chiefly from Mr. Hunter's *Life of Lord Mayo.*

APPENDIX XI.

The various changes made in direct taxation during the last twenty years may be seen in the following list:—

1860. Income-tax of 3 per cent.
1861. License-tax.
1863. Income-tax reduced.
1866. The previous Acts came to an end.
1867–8. License-tax for all India (1) on incomes as low as 200 rupees, (2) on minimum of 500.
1869. Income-tax of 1–2½ per cent.
1870. New Income-tax of 3 per cent.
1871. Further changes made in its assessment.
1872. The minimum was raised.
1873. It expired.
1877. A license-tax.

1879. Changes made in Bengal.

1880. The minimum raised to 500 rupees.

When it is remembered that all these changes have been made within twenty years, and every method tried to get at fair assessments, it is not surprising that natives are very shy of showing any signs of wealth. They are not likely to invest in State loans or spend any money on agricultural improvements, such as wells, when they know that the Government official has his eye on them. The agriculturist has, under the License-tax Act, been taxed as a grain-dealer. He has also the land-cess to pay.

'The primitive notion of taxation is, that when a Government sees much money, it should take some of it, and if it sees more money it should take more of it.' This remark of W. Bagehot is fully substantiated by the policy of the Indian Government. If, under native rule, the trader was to be taxed, the custom was to levy a lump sum on each bazaar and let the tradesmen settle it among themselves. But we are above sending the hat round.

APPENDIX XII.

On the 4th of October, 1877, the Government of the North-West Provinces and Oudh reported as follows to the Government of India, 'on the condition and agricultural prospects' of the provinces under its administration: 'Since the latter date (September 11) there has been no rain anywhere, and the whole of the provinces has been devastated by a hot dry wind. . . . The consequences of this disastrous failure of the usual rains are most deplorable for man and beast. The full effect cannot yet be determined; but it is now certain that in Meerut, Agra, Rohilkhund, Sitapur, and Lucknow divisions, and in parts of the Allahabad, Jhansi, Rae-Bareli, and Fyzabad divisions the unirrigated crops are entirely destroyed. In Benares and greater part of Allahabad and Fyzabad it was hoped, after the rain of the 10th and 11th, that from five to eight annas (i.e. a third to one-half) would be saved; but these hopes it is now known cannot be realised. The hot wind that has raged since the 11th has irretrievably damaged much that survived, and threatens to destroy all. A speedy fall of rain would save some; and in part of the Jhansi division there is also a little which is not yet utterly ruined. . . . The general result is as stated above, that, except in parts of Benares, Fyzabad, and Allahabad, the outturn of the unirrigated *Kharif* (i.e. cold-weather crop) will be *nil.* Unfortunately, the area of irrigated *Kharif* is very small. . . . Food grains and fodder are generally grown on lands that depend on the periodical rainfall, and at the sowing season the cultivators could not foresee the terrible drought that was to prevail, and did not avail themselves of canal water for this class of crop. . . One of the most deplorable consequences of the failure of the *Kharif* is the inevitable great mortality among cattle for want of fodder, and that too at a time when the need for well irrigation is most pressing. . . . Loss of cattle from starvation has been reported, and there is no means of providing sustenance for them. . . . It has been with some certainty ascertained that what grain there is in the provinces is chiefly in the hands of dealers, and that the stocks held by cultivators and others are low. . . . Prices are now in the worst places more than double what they were three months ago. They verge on famine rates.'

A week later the Local Government made the following appeal to the Government of India : 'The Lieutenant-Governor is well aware of the straits to which the Government of India is put at the present time for money, and it is with the utmost reluctance that he makes a report which must necessarily temporarily add to their burdens. But he sees no other course to adopt. If the village communities who form the great mass of our revenue-payers be pressed now, they will simply be ruined, whereas, if we allow temporary suspension there is every reason to believe that by the end of the agricultural year we shall recover all that we forego now, from the proceeds of the additional area which the people will be able to bring under cultivation in consequence of the *Kharif* not having been sown, and the land being available for the spring sowings. But, if we press for immediate payment, the people will not have the means of doing this, and they will be reduced to such a state that the rabi (i.e. the spring) instalments themselves will only be realised with difficulty.' These statements are taken from an article written by Col. R. D. Osborn in the *Contemporary Review* of February, 1880. The extracts from official documents have not been disputed.

According to the Indian Famine Commission's Report, 'about a quarter of the land revenue (or 46 lakhs of rupees) was suspended at the end of 1877, but when the spring harvest turned out a good one, the Government ordered the arrears to be got in as far as possible, and by the time the autumn crop was ripe the collection was deficient by about 12 lakhs only' (46 lakhs are not $\frac{1}{4}$, but $\frac{1}{6}$th of 280 lakhs). The excess number of deaths is calculated at 1,250,000. 'Small-pox, fever, and bowel diseases were the chief registered causes, and these epidemics were extremely virulent, but doubtless a large portion of the deaths was due to the pressure of want.'

I have shown in the text that the Government of these Provinces admits in its report that the suspensions were not sufficient, and it is obvious from the Commission's report that arrears were very soon collected. Colonel Osborn further quotes from Auckland Colvin, late Collector of Bijnour, and now in the service of the Khedive of Egypt, as saying that in spite of the relief afforded by the suspension of half the demand in his district, 'money had to be borrowed on a large scale at a high rate of interest, and much jewellery was sold or pawned. Registered deeds show a very heavy increase, and so do transfers of property. A calamity such as that of 1877-78, partial though it was, guts a district; embarrasments have been renewed or created, which will never be cleared off.'

When I was in these Provinces, I certainly found it to be the general opinion that there had been great distress caused by the collection of land-revenue.

The famine was not really over till the autumn, and yet arrears were collected after the spring harvest. 'The spring harvest,' write the Famine Commissioners, 'again offered employment in March 1878, and the people left the relief works in large crowds *to return again in May, and to increase in numbers and despondency*, as the rains again showed signs of holding off in June and July. In August, however, there was a plentiful downfall, which secured the (i.e. autumn) harvest. . . . . The highest number on relief works was in August, 126,800, and in the same month the number in the poor-houses also reached its maximum of 26,350.' It is also stated (para. 60), the calamitous season of 1877 was accompanied by an extremely high range of prices over all India, due parity to the deficient harvest, and partly to the reduction of the food stock through export from the Northern Provinces to the South and to Europe.'

The railways paid splendidly with all this traffic in grain, first southwards and then northwards, but the people died. There are two lines of railway running through the North-Western Provinces and Oudh, so that more railways would not appear to meet the difficulty.

A LIST OF

C. KEGAN PAUL AND CO.'S

PUBLICATIONS.

A LIST OF C. KEGAN PAUL AND CO.'S PUBLICATIONS.

ADAMS (F. O.), F.R.G.S.

The History of Japan. From the Earliest Period to the Present Time. New Edition, revised. 2 volumes. With Maps and Plans. Demy 8vo. Cloth, price 21*s.* each.

ADAMS (W. D.).

Lyrics of Love, from Shakespeare to Tennyson. Selected and arranged by. Fcap. 8vo. Cloth extra, gilt edges, price 3*s.* 6*d.*

Also, a Cheap Edition. Fcap. 8vo. Cloth, price 2*s.* 6*d.*

ADAMSON H. T.), B.D.

The Truth as it is in Jesus. Crown 8vo. Cloth, price 8*s.* 6*d.*

A. K. H. B.

From a Quiet Place. A New Volume of Sermons. Crown 8vo. Cloth, price 5*s.*

ALBERT (Mary).

Holland and her Heroes to the year 1585. An Adaptation from Motley's "Rise of the Dutch Republic." Small crown 8vo. Cloth, price, 4*s.* 6*d.*

ALLEN (Rev. R.), M.A.

Abraham; his Life, Times, and Travels, 3,800 years ago. Second Edition. With Map. Post 8vo. Cloth, price 6*s.*

ALLEN (Grant), B.A.

Physiological Æsthetics. Large post 8vo. 9*s.*

ALLIES (T. W.), M.A.

Per Crucem ad Lucem. The Result of a Life. 2 vols. Demy 8vo. Cloth, price 25*s.*

A Life's Decision. Crown 8vo. Cloth, price 7*s.* 6*d.*

AMATEUR.

A Few Lyrics. Small crown 8vo. Cloth, price 2*s.*

AMOS (Prof. Sheldon).

Science of Law. Fourth Edition. Crown 8vo. Cloth, price 5*s.*

Volume X. of The International Scientific Series.

ANDERSON (Col. R. P.).

Victories and Defeats. An Attempt to explain the Causes which have led to them. An Officer's Manual. Demy 8vo. Cloth, price 14*s.*

ANDERSON (R. C.), C.E.

Tables for Facilitating the Calculation of every Detail in connection with Earthen and Masonry Dams. Royal 8vo. Cloth, price £2 2*s.*

Antiope. A Tragedy. Large crown 8vo. Cloth, price 6*s.*

ARCHER (Thomas).

About my Father's Business. Work amidst the Sick, the Sad, and the Sorrowing. Crown 8vo. Cloth, price 2*s.* 6*d.*

Army of the North German Confederation.

A Brief Description of its Organization, of the Different Branches of the Service and their *rôle* in War, of its Mode of Fighting, &c. &c. Translated from the Corrected Edition, by permission of the Author, by Colonel Edward Newdigate. Demy 8vo. Cloth, price 5*s.*

ARNOLD (Arthur).

Social Politics. Demy 8vo. Cloth, price 14*s.*

Free Land. Crown 8vo. Cloth, price 6*s.*

AUBERTIN (J. J.).

Camoens' Lusiads. Portuguese Text, with Translation by. With Map and Portraits. 2 vols. Demy 8vo. Price 30*s.*

Aunt Mary's Bran Pie.

By the author of "St. Olave's." Illustrated. Cloth, price 3*s.* 6*d.*

AVIA.

The Odyssey of Homer Done into English Verse. Fcap. 4to. Cloth, price 15*s.*

BAGEHOT (Walter).

Physics and Politics; or, Thoughts on the Application of the Principles of "Natural Selection" and "Inheritance" to Political Society. Fifth Edition. Crown 8vo. Cloth, price 4*s.*

Volume II. of The International Scientific Series.

Some Articles on the Depreciation of Silver, and Topics connected with it. Demy 8vo. Price 5*s.*

The English Constitution. A New Edition, Revised and Corrected, with an Introductory Dissertation on Recent Changes and Events. Crown 8vo. Cloth, price 7*s.* 6*d.*

Lombard Street. A Description of the Money Market. Seventh Edition. Crown 8vo. Cloth, price 7*s.* 6*d.*

BAGOT (Alan).

Accidents in Mines: their Causes and Prevention. Crown 8vo. Cloth, price 6*s.*

BAIN (Alexander), LL.D.

Mind and Body: the Theories of their relation. Seventh Edition. Crown 8vo. Cloth, price 4*s.*

Volume IV. of The International Scientific Series.

Education as a Science. Crown 8vo. Third Edition. Cloth, price 5*s.*

Volume XXV. of The International Scientific Series.

BAKER (Sir Sherston, Bart.).

Halleck's International Law; or Rules Regulating the Intercourse of States in Peace and War. A New Edition, Revised, with Notes and Cases. 2 vols. Demy 8vo. Cloth, price 38*s.*

The Laws relating to Quarantine. Crown 8vo. Cloth, price 12*s.* 6*d.*

BALDWIN (Capt. J. H.), F.Z.S.

The Large and Small Game of Bengal and the North-Western Provinces of India. 4to. With numerous Illustrations. Second Edition. Cloth, price 21*s.*

BANKS (Mrs. G. L.).

God's Providence House. New Edition. Crown 8vo. Cloth, price 3*s.* 6*d.*

Ripples and Breakers. Poems. Square 8vo. Cloth, price 5*s.*

BARLEE (Ellen).

Locked Out: a Tale of the Strike. With a Frontispiece. Royal 16mo. Cloth, price 1*s.* 6*d.*

BARNES (William).

An Outline of English Speechcraft. Crown 8vo. Cloth, price 4*s.*

Poems of Rural Life, in the Dorset Dialect. New Edition, complete in 1 vol. Crown 8vo. Cloth, price 8*s.* 6*d.*

Outlines of Redecraft (Logic). With English Wording. Crown 8vo. Cloth, price 3*s.*

BARTLEY (George C. T.).

Domestic Economy: Thrift in Every Day Life. Taught in Dialogues suitable for Children of all ages. Small crown 8vo. Cloth, limp, 2*s.*

BASTIAN (H. Charlton), M.D.

The Brain as an Organ of Mind. With numerous Illustrations. Second Edition. Crown 8vo. Cloth, price 5*s.*

Volume XXIX. of the International Scientific Series.

BAUR (Ferdinand), Dr. Ph.
A Philological Introduction to Greek and Latin for Students. Translated and adapted from the German of. By C. Kegan Paul, M.A. Oxon., and the Rev. E. D. Stone, M.A., late Fellow of King's College, Cambridge, and Assistant Master at Eton. Second and revised edition. Crown 8vo. Cloth, price 6*s*.

BAYNES (Rev. Canon R. H.)
At the Communion Time. A Manual for Holy Communion. With a preface by the Right Rev. the Lord Bishop of Derry and Raphoe. Cloth, price 1*s*. 6*d*.

*** Can also be had bound in French morocco, price 2*s*. 6*d*.; Persian morocco, price 3*s*.; Calf, or Turkey morocco, price 3*s*. 6*d*.

Home Songs for Quiet Hours. Fourth and cheaper Edition. Fcap. 8vo. Cloth, price 2*s*. 6*d*.
This may also be had handsomely bound in morocco with gilt edges.

BELLINGHAM (Henry), Barrister-at-Law.
Social Aspects of Catholicism and Protestantism in their Civil Bearing upon Nations. Translated and adapted from the French of M. le Baron de Haulleville. With a Preface by His Eminence Cardinal Manning. Crown 8vo. Cloth, price 6*s*.

BENNETT (Dr. W. C.).
Narrative Poems & Ballads. Fcap. 8vo. Sewed in Coloured Wrapper, price 1*s*.

Songs for Sailors. Dedicated by Special Request to H. R. H. the Duke of Edinburgh. With Steel Portrait and Illustrations. Crown 8vo. Cloth, price 3*s*. 6*d*.

An Edition in Illustrated Paper Covers, price 1*s*.

Songs of a Song Writer. Crown 8vo. Cloth, price 6*s*.

BERNSTEIN (Prof.).
The Five Senses of Man. With 91 Illustrations. Second Edition. Crown 8vo. Cloth, price 5*s*.
Volume XXI. of The International Scientific Series.

BETHAM - EDWARDS (Miss M.).
Kitty. With a Frontispiece. Crown 8vo. Cloth, price 6*s*.

BEVINGTON (L. S.).
Key Notes. Small crown 8vo. Cloth, price 5*s*.

BLASERNA (Prof. Pietro).
The Theory of Sound in its Relation to Music. With numerous Illustrations. Second Edition. Crown 8vo. Cloth, price 5*s*.
Volume XXII. of The International Scientific Series.

Blue Roses; or, Helen Malinofska's Marriage. By the Author of "Véra." 2 vols. Fifth Edition. Cloth, gilt tops, 12*s*.

*** Also a Cheaper Edition in 1 vol. With Frontispiece. Crown 8vo. Cloth, price 6*s*.

BLUME (Major W.).
The Operations of the German Armies in France, from Sedan to the end of the war of 1870-71. With Map. From the Journals of the Head-quarters Staff. Translated by the late E. M. Jones, Maj. 20th Foot, Prof. of Mil. Hist., Sandhurst. Demy 8vo. Cloth, price 9*s*.

BOGUSLAWSKI (Capt. A. von).
Tactical Deductions from the War of 1870-71. Translated by Colonel Sir Lumley Graham, Bart., late 18th (Royal Irish) Regiment. Third Edition, Revised and Corrected. Demy 8vo. Cloth, price 7*s*.

BONWICK (J.), F.R.G.S.
Egyptian Belief and Modern Thought. Large post 8vo. Cloth, price 10*s*. 6*d*.

Pyramid Facts and Fancies. Crown 8vo. Cloth, price 5*s*.

The Tasmanian Lily. With Frontispiece. Crown 8vo. Cloth, price 5*s*.

Mike Howe, the Bushranger of Van Diemen's Land. With Frontispiece. Crown. 8vo. Cloth, price 5*s*.

BOWEN (H. C.), M. A.

English Grammar for Beginners. Fcap. 8vo. Cloth, price 1*s.*

Studies in English, for the use of Modern Schools. Small crown 8vo. Cloth, price 1*s.* 6*d.*

Simple English Poems. English Literature for Junior Classes. In Four Parts. Parts I. and II., price 6*d.* each, now ready.

BOWRING (Sir John).

Autobiographical Recollections. With Memoir by Lewin B. Bowring. Demy 8vo. Price 14*s.*

Brave Men's Footsteps.

By the Editor of "Men who have Risen." A Book of Example and Anecdote for Young People. With Four Illustrations by C. Doyle. Sixth Edition. Crown 8vo. Cloth, price 3*s.* 6*d.*

BRIALMONT (Col. A.).

Hasty Intrenchments. Translated by Lieut. Charles A. Empson, R.A. With Nine Plates. Demy 8vo. Cloth, price 6*s.*

BRODRICK (The Hon. G. C.).

Political Studies. Demy 8vo. Cloth, price 14*s.*

BROOKE (Rev. S. A.), M. A.

The Late Rev. F. W. Robertson, M.A., Life and Letters of. Edited by.

I. Uniform with the Sermons. 2 vols. With Steel Portrait. Price 7*s.* 6*d.*

II. Library Edition. 8vo. With Two Steel Portraits. Price 12*s.*

III. A Popular Edition, in 1 vol. 8vo. Price 6*s.*

Theology in the English Poets. — COWPER, COLERIDGE, WORDSWORTH, and BURNS. New and Cheaper Edition. Post 8vo. Cloth, price 5*s.*

Christ in Modern Life. Fourteenth and Cheaper Edition. Crown 8vo. Cloth, price 5*s.*

Sermons. First Series. Eleventh Edition. Crown 8vo. Cloth, price 6*s.*

BROOKE (Rev. S. A.), M.A.—*continued.*

Sermons. Second Series. Third Edition. Crown 8vo. Cloth, price 7*s.*

The Fight of Faith. Sermons preached on various occasions. Third Edition. Crown 8vo. Cloth, price 7*s.* 6*d.*

Frederick Denison Maurice: The Life and Work of. A Memorial Sermon. Crown 8vo. Sewed, price 1*s.*

BROOKE (W. G.), M.A.

The Public Worship Regulation Act. With a Classified Statement of its Provisions, Notes, and Index. Third Edition, Revised and Corrected. Crown 8vo. Cloth, price 3*s.* 6*d.*

Six Privy Council Judgments—1850-1872. Annotated by. Third Edition. Crown 8vo. Cloth, price 9*s.*

BROUN (J. A.).

Magnetic Observations at Trevandrum and Augustia Malley. Vol. I. 4to. Cloth, price 63*s.*

The Report from above, separately sewed, price 21*s.*

BROWN (Rev. J. Baldwin).

The Higher Life. Its Reality, Experience, and Destiny. Fifth and Cheaper Edition. Crown 8vo. Cloth, price 5*s.*

Doctrine of Annihilation in the Light of the Gospel of Love. Five Discourses. Third Edition. Crown 8vo. Cloth, price 2*s.* 6*d.*

The Christian Policy of Life. A Book for Young Men of Business. New and Cheaper Edition. Crown 8vo. Cloth, price 3*s.* 6*d.*

BROWN (J. Croumbie), LL.D.

Reboisement in France; or, Records of the Replanting of the Alps, the Cevennes, and the Pyrenees with Trees, Herbage, and Bush. Demy 8vo. Cloth, price 12*s.* 6*d.*

The Hydrology of Southern Africa. Demy 8vo. Cloth, price 10*s.* 6*d.*

BRYANT (W. C.)

Poems. Red-line Edition. With 24 Illustrations and Portrait of the Author. Crown 8vo. Cloth extra, price 7*s*. 6*d*.

A Cheaper Edition, with Frontispiece. Small crown 8vo. Cloth, price 3*s*. 6*d*.

BURCKHARDT (Jacob).

The Civilization of the Period of the Renaissance in Italy. Authorized translation, by S. G. C. Middlemore. 2 vols. Demy 8vo. Cloth, price 24*s*.

BURTON (Mrs. Richard).

The Inner Life of Syria, Palestine, and the Holy Land. With Maps, Photographs, and Coloured Plates. 2 vols. Second Edition. Demy 8vo. Cloth, price 24*s*.

*** Also a Cheaper Edition in one volume. Large post 8vo. Cloth, price 10*s*. 6*d*.

BURTON (Capt. Richard F.).

The Gold Mines of Midian and the Ruined Midianite Cities. A Fortnight's Tour in North Western Arabia. With numerous Illustrations. Second Edition. Demy 8vo. Cloth, price 18*s*.

The Land of Midian Revisited. With numerous illustrations on wood and by Chromolithography. 2 vols. Demy 8vo. Cloth, price 32*s*.

CALDERON.

Calderon's Dramas: The Wonder-Working Magician—Life is a Dream—The Purgatory of St. Patrick. Translated by Denis Florence MacCarthy. Post 8vo. Cloth, price 10*s*.

CANDLER (H.).

The Groundwork of Belief. Crown 8vo. Cloth, price 7*s*.

CARPENTER (W. B.), M.D.

The Principles of Mental Physiology. With their Applications to the Training and Discipline of the Mind, and the Study of its Morbid Conditions. Illustrated. Fifth Edition. 8vo. Cloth, price 12*s*.

CAVALRY OFFICER.

Notes on Cavalry Tactics, Organization, &c. With Diagrams. Demy 8vo. Cloth, price 12*s*.

CHAPMAN (Hon. Mrs. E. W.).

A Constant Heart. A Story. 2 vols. Cloth, gilt tops, price 12*s*.

CHEYNE (Rev. T. K.).

The Prophecies of Isaiah. Translated, with Critical Notes and Dissertations by. Two vols., demy 8vo. Cloth. Vol. I., price 12*s*. 6*d*.

Children's Toys, and some Elementary Lessons in General Knowledge which they teach. Illustrated. Crown 8vo. Cloth, price 5*s*.

CHRISTOPHERSON (The late Rev. Henry), M.A.

Sermons. With an Introduction by John Rae, LL.D., F.S.A. Second Series. Crown 8vo. Cloth, price 6*s*.

CLAYDEN (P. W.).

England under Lord Beaconsfield. The Political History of the Last Six Years, from the end of 1873 to the beginning of 1880. Second Edition. With Index, and Continuation to March, 1880. Demy 8vo. Cloth, price 16*s*.

CLERY (C.), Major.

Minor Tactics. With 26 Maps and Plans. Fourth and Revised Edition. Demy 8vo. Cloth, price 16*s*.

CLODD (Edward), F.R.A.S.

The Childhood of the World: a Simple Account of Man in Early Times. Sixth Edition. Crown 8vo. Cloth, price 3*s*.

A Special Edition for Schools. Price 1*s*.

The Childhood of Religions. Including a Simple Account of the Birth and Growth of Myths and Legends. Third Thousand. Crown 8vo. Cloth, price 5*s*.

A Special Edition for Schools. Price 1*s*. 6*d*.

Jesus of Nazareth. With a brief Sketch of Jewish History to the Time of His Birth. Small crown 8vo. Cloth, price 6*s*.

COLERIDGE (Sara).

Pretty Lessons in Verse for Good Children, with some Lessons in Latin, in Easy Rhyme. A New Edition. Illustrated. Fcap. 8vo. Cloth, price 3*s.* 6*d.*

Phantasmion. A Fairy Tale. With an Introductory Preface by the Right Hon. Lord Coleridge, of Ottery St. Mary. A New Edition. Illustrated. Crown 8vo. Cloth, price 7*s.* 6*d.*

Memoir and Letters of Sara Coleridge. Edited by her Daughter. Cheap Edition. With one Portrait. Cloth, price 7*s.* 6*d.*

COLLINS (Mortimer).

The Secret of Long Life. Small crown 8vo. Cloth, price 3*s.* 6*d.*

Inn of Strange Meetings, and other Poems. Crown 8vo. Cloth, price 5*s.*

CONWAY (Hugh).

A Life's Idylls. Small crown 8vo. Cloth, price 3*s.* 6*d.*

COOKE (M. C.), M.A., LL.D.

Fungi; their Nature, Influences, Uses, &c. Edited by the Rev. M. J. Berkeley, M.A., F.L.S. With Illustrations. Second Edition. Crown 8vo. Cloth, price 5*s.*

Volume XIV. of The International Scientific Series.

COOKE (Prof. J. P.)

The New Chemistry. With 31 Illustrations. Fifth Edition. Crown 8vo. Cloth, price 5*s.*

Volume IX. of The International Scientific Series.

Scientific Culture. Crown 8vo. Cloth, price 1*s.*

COOPER (H. J.).

The Art of Furnishing on Rational and Æsthetic Principles. New and Cheaper Edition. Fcap. 8vo. Cloth, price 1*s.* 6*d.*

COPPÉE (François).

L'Exilée. Done into English Verse with the sanction of the Author by I. O. L. Crown 8vo. Vellum, price 5*s.*

CORFIELD (Prof.), M.D.

Health. Crown 8vo. Cloth, price 6*s.*

CORY (William).

A Guide to Modern English History. Part I. MDCCCXV.—MDCCCXXX. Demy 8vo. Cloth, price 9*s.*

COURTNEY (W. L.).

The Metaphysics of John Stuart Mill. Crown 8vo. Cloth, price 5*s.* 6*d.*

COWAN (Rev. William).

Poems: Chiefly Sacred, including Translations from some Ancient Latin Hymns. Fcap. 8vo. Cloth, price 5*s.*

COX (Rev. Sir G. W.), Bart.

A History of Greece from the Earliest Period to the end of the Persian War. New Edition. 2 vols. Demy 8vo. Cloth, price 36*s.*

The Mythology of the Aryan Nations. New Edition. 2 vols. Demy 8vo. Cloth, price 28*s.*

A General History of Greece from the Earliest Period to the Death of Alexander the Great, with a sketch of the subsequent History to the present time. New Edition. Crown 8vo. Cloth, price 7*s.* 6*d.*

Tales of Ancient Greece. New Edition. Small crown 8vo. Cloth, price 6*s.*

School History of Greece. With Maps. New Edition. Fcap. 8vo. Cloth, price 3*s.* 6*d.*

The Great Persian War from the Histories of Herodotus. New Edition. Fcap. 8vo. Cloth, price 3*s.* 6*d.*

A Manual of Mythology in the form of Question and Answer. New Edition. Fcap. 8vo. Cloth, price 3*s.*

COX (Rev. Sir G. W.), Bart., M.A., and EUSTACE HINTON JONES.

Popular Romances of the Middle Ages. Second Edition in one volume. Crown 8vo. Cloth, price 6*s.*

COX (Rev. Samuel).

Salvator Mundi; or, Is Christ the Saviour of all Men? Sixth Edition. Crown 8vo. Cloth, price 5*s.*

The Genesis of Evil, and other Sermons, mainly Expository. Second Edition. Crown 8vo. Cloth, price 6*s.*

CRAUFURD (A. H.).

Seeking for Light: Sermons. Crown 8vo. Cloth, price 5*s.*

CRAWFURD (Oswald).

Portugal, Old and New. With Illustrations and Maps. Demy 8vo. Cloth, price 16*s.*

CRESSWELL (Mrs. G.).

The King's Banner. Drama in Four Acts. Five Illustrations. 4to. Cloth, price 10*s.* 6*d.*

CROMPTON (Henry).

Industrial Conciliation. Fcap. 8vo. Cloth, price 2*s.* 6*d.*

CROZIER (John Beattie), M.B.

The Religion of the Future. Crown 8vo. Cloth, price 6*s.*

D'ANVERS (N. R.).

Parted. A Tale of Clouds and Sunshine. With 4 Illustrations. Extra Fcap. 8vo. Cloth, price 3*s.* 6*d.*

Little Minnie's Troubles. An Every-day Chronicle. With Four Illustrations by W. H. Hughes. Fcap. Cloth, price 3*s.* 6*d.*

Pixie's Adventures; or, the Tale of a Terrier. With 21 Illustrations. 16mo. Cloth, price 4*s.* 6*d.*

Nanny's Adventures; or, the Tale of a Goat. With 12 Illustrations. 16mo. Cloth, price 4*s.* 6*d.*

DAVIDSON (Rev. Samuel), D.D., LL.D.

The New Testament, translated from the Latest Greek Text of Tischendorf. A New and thoroughly Revised Edition. Post 8vo. Cloth, price 10*s.* 6*d.*

DAVIDSON (Rev. Samuel), D.D., LL.D.—*continued.*

Canon of the Bible: Its Formation, History, and Fluctuations. Third Edition, revised and enlarged. Small crown 8vo. Cloth, price 5*s.*

DAVIES (G. Christopher).

Rambles and Adventures of Our School Field Club. With Four Illustrations. Crown 8vo. Cloth, price 5*s.*

DAVIES (Rev. J. L.), M.A.

Theology and Morality. Essays on Questions of Belief and Practice. Crown 8vo. Cloth, price 7*s.* 6*d.*

DAVIES (T. Hart.).

Catullus. Translated into English Verse. Crown 8vo. Cloth, price 6*s.*

DAWSON (George), M.A.

Prayers, with a Discourse on Prayer. Edited by his Wife. Fifth Edition. Crown 8vo. Price 6*s.*

Sermons on Disputed Points and Special Occasions. Edited by his Wife. Third Edition. Crown 8vo. Cloth, price 6*s.*

Sermons on Daily Life and Duty. Edited by his Wife. Second Edition. Crown 8vo. Cloth, price 6*s.*

DE L'HOSTE (Col. E. P.).

The Desert Pastor, Jean Jarousseau. Translated from the French of Eugène Pelletan. With a Frontispiece. New Edition. Fcap. 8vo. Cloth, price 3*s.* 6*d.*

DENNIS (J.).

English Sonnets. Collected and Arranged. Elegantly bound. Fcap. 8vo. Cloth, price 3*s.* 6*d.*

DE REDCLIFFE (Viscount Stratford), P.C., K.G., G.C.B.

Why am I a Christian? Fifth Edition. Crown 8vo. Cloth, price 3*s.*

DESPREZ (Philip S.).

Daniel and John; or, the Apocalypse of the Old and that of the New Testament. Demy 8vo. Cloth, price 12*s.*

DE TOCQUEVILLE (A.).

Correspondence and Conversations of, with Nassau William Senior, from 1834 to 1859. Edited by M. C. M. Simpson. 2 vols. Post 8vo. Cloth, price 21*s*.

DE VERE (Aubrey).

Legends of the Saxon Saints. Small crown 8vo. Cloth, price 6*s*.

Alexander the Great. A Dramatic Poem. Small crown 8vo. Cloth, price 5*s*.

The Infant Bridal, and other Poems. A New and Enlarged Edition. Fcap. 8vo. Cloth, price 7*s*. 6*d*.

The Legends of St. Patrick, and other Poems. Small crown 8vo. Cloth, price 5*s*.

St. Thomas of Canterbury. A Dramatic Poem. Large fcap. 8vo. Cloth, price 5*s*.

Antar and Zara: an Eastern Romance. INISFAIL, and other Poems, Meditative and Lyrical. Fcap. 8vo. Price 6*s*.

The Fall of Rora, the Search after Proserpine, and other Poems, Meditative and Lyrical. Fcap. 8vo. Price 6*s*.

DOBSON (Austin).

Vignettes in Rhyme and Vers de Société. Third Edition. Fcap. 8vo. Cloth, price 5*s*.

Proverbs in Porcelain. By the Author of "Vignettes in Rhyme." Second Edition. Crown 8vo. 6*s*.

DOWDEN (Edward), LL.D.

Shakspere: a Critical Study of his Mind and Art. Fifth Edition. Large post 8vo. Cloth, price 12*s*.

Studies in Literature, 1789-1877. Large post 8vo. Cloth, price 12*s*.

Poems. Second Edition. Fcap. 8vo. Cloth, price 5*s*.

DOWNTON (Rev. H.), M.A.

Hymns and Verses. Original and Translated. Small crown 8vo. Cloth, price 3*s*. 6*d*.

DRAPER (J. W.), M.D., LL.D.

History of the Conflict between Religion and Science. Fourteenth Edition. Crown 8vo. Cloth, price 5*s*.

Volume XIII. of The International Scientific Series.

DREW (Rev. G. S.), M.A.

Scripture Lands in connection with their History. Second Edition. 8vo. Cloth, price 10*s*. 6*d*.

Nazareth: Its Life and Lessons. Third Edition. Crown 8vo. Cloth, price 5*s*.

The Divine Kingdom on Earth as it is in Heaven. 8vo. Cloth, price 10*s*. 6*d*.

The Son of Man: His Life and Ministry. Crown 8vo. Cloth price 7*s*. 6*d*.

DREWRY (G. O.), M.D.

The Common-Sense Management of the Stomach. Fifth Edition. Fcap. 8vo. Cloth, price 2*s*. 6*d*.

DREWRY (G. O.), M.D., and BARTLETT (H. C.), Ph.D., F.C.S.

Cup and Platter: or, Notes on Food and its Effects. New and cheaper Edition. Small 8vo. Cloth, price 1*s*. 6*d*.

DRUMMOND (Miss).

Tripps Buildings. A Study from Life, with Frontispiece. Small crown 8vo. Cloth, price 3*s*. 6*d*.

DU MONCEL (Count).

The Telephone, the Microphone, and the Phonograph. With 74 Illustrations. Small crown 8vo. Cloth, price 5*s*.

DU VERNOIS (Col. von Verdy).

Studies in leading Troops. An authorized and accurate Translation by Lieutenant H. J. T. Hildyard, 71st Foot. Parts I. and II. Demy 8vo. Cloth, price 7*s*.

EDEN (Frederick).

The Nile without a Dragoman. Second Edition. Crown 8vo. Cloth, price 7*s*. 6*d*.

A 2

EDMONDS (Herbert).

Well Spent Lives: a Series of Modern Biographies. Crown 8vo. Price 5*s*.

Educational Code of the Prussian Nation, in its Present Form. In accordance with the Decisions of the Common Provincial Law, and with those of Recent Legislation. Crown 8vo. Cloth, price 2*s*. 6*d*.

EDWARDS (Rev. Basil).

Minor Chords; or, Songs for the Suffering: a Volume of Verse. Fcap. 8vo. Cloth, price 3*s*. 6*d*.; paper, price 2*s*. 6*d*.

ELLIOT (Lady Charlotte).

Medusa and other Poems. Crown 8vo. Cloth, price 6*s*.

ELLIOTT (Ebenezer), The Corn-Law Rhymer.

Poems. Edited by his Son, the Rev. Edwin Elliott, of St. John's, Antigua. 2 vols. Crown 8vo. Cloth, price 18*s*.

ELSDALE (Henry).

Studies in Tennyson's Idylls. Crown 8vo. Cloth, price 5*s*.

Epic of Hades (The). By the author of "Songs of Two Worlds." Tenth and finally revised Edition. Fcap. 8vo. Cloth, price 7*s*. 6*d*.

*** Also an Illustrated Edition with seventeen full-page designs in photo-mezzotint by GEORGE R. CHAPMAN. 4to. Cloth, extra gilt leaves, price 25*s*.

EVANS (Mark).

The Gospel of Home Life. Crown 8vo. Cloth, price 4*s*. 6*d*.

The Story of our Father's Love, told to Children. Fourth and Cheaper Edition. With Four Illustrations. Fcap. 8vo. Cloth, price 1*s*. 6*d*.

A Book of Common Prayer and Worship for Household Use, compiled exclusively from the Holy Scriptures. New and Cheaper Edition. Fcap. 8vo. Cloth, price 1*s*.

EVANS (Mark)—*continued*.

The King's Story Book. In three parts. Fcap. 8vo. Cloth, price 1*s*. 6*d*. each.

*** Part I., with four illustrations and Picture Map, now ready.

EX-CIVILIAN.

Life in the Mofussil; or, Civilian Life in Lower Bengal. 2 vols. Large post 8vo. Price 14*s*.

FARQUHARSON (M.).

I. Elsie Dinsmore. Crown 8vo. Cloth, price 3*s*. 6*d*.

II. Elsie's Girlhood. Crown 8vo. Cloth, price 3*s*. 6*d*.

III. Elsie's Holidays at Roselands. Crown 8vo. Cloth, price 3*s*. 6*d*.

FIELD (Horace), B.A. Lond.

The Ultimate Triumph of Christianity. Small crown 8vo. Cloth, price 3*s*. 6*d*.

FINN (the late James), M.R.A.S.

Stirring Times; or, Records from Jerusalem Consular Chronicles of 1853 to 1856. Edited and Compiled by his Widow. With a Preface by the Viscountess STRANGFORD. 2 vols. Demy 8vo. Price 30*s*.

Folkestone Ritual Case (The). The Argument, Proceedings, Judgment, and Report, revised by the several Counsel engaged. Demy 8vo. Cloth, price 25*s*.

FORMBY (Rev. Henry).

Ancient Rome and its Connection with the Christian Religion: an Outline of the History of the City from its First Foundation down to the Erection of the Chair of St. Peter, A.D. 42-47. With numerous Illustrations of Ancient Monuments, Sculpture, and Coinage, and of the Antiquities of the Christian Catacombs. Royal 4to. Cloth extra, price 50*s*. Roxburgh, half-morocco, price 52*s*. 6*d*.

FOWLE (Rev. Edmund).

Latin Primer Rules made Easy. Crown 8vo. Cloth, price 3*s*.

FOWLE (Rev. T. W.), M.A.

The Reconciliation of Religion and Science. Being Essays on Immortality, Inspiration, Miracles, and the Being of Christ. Demy 8vo. Cloth, price 10*s.* 6*d.*

The Divine Legation of Christ. Crown 8vo. Cloth, price 7*s.*

FRASER (Donald).

Exchange Tables of Sterling and Indian Rupee Currency, upon a new and extended system, embracing Values from One Farthing to One Hundred Thousand Pounds, and at Rates progressing, in Sixteenths of a Penny, from 1*s.* 9*d.* to 2*s.* 3*d.* per Rupee. Royal 8vo. Cloth, price 10*s.* 6*d.*

FRISWELL (J. Hain).

The Better Self. Essays for Home Life. Crown 8vo. Cloth, price 6*s.*

One of Two; or, A Left-Handed Bride. With a Frontispiece. Crown 8vo. Cloth, price 3*s.* 6*d.*

GARDNER (J.), M.D.

Longevity: The Means of Prolonging Life after Middle Age. Fourth Edition, Revised and Enlarged. Small crown 8vo. Cloth, price 4*s.*

GARRETT (E.).

By Still Waters. A Story for Quiet Hours. With Seven Illustrations. Crown 8vo. Cloth, price 6*s.*

GEBLER (Karl Von).

Galileo Galilei and the Roman Curia, from Authentic Sources. Translated with the sanction of the Author, by Mrs. George Sturge. Demy 8vo. Cloth, price 12*s.*

GEDDES (James).

History of the Administration of John de Witt, Grand Pensionary of Holland. Vol. I. 1623—1654. Demy 8vo., with Portrait. Cloth, price 15*s.*

G. H. T.

Verses, mostly written in India. Crown 8vo. Cloth, price 6*s.*

GILBERT (Mrs.).

Autobiography and other Memorials. Edited by Josiah Gilbert. Third Edition. With Portrait and several Wood Engravings. Crown 8vo. Cloth, price 7*s.* 6*d.*

GILL (Rev. W. W.), B.A.

Myths and Songs from the South Pacific. With a Preface by F. Max Müller, M.A., Professor of Comparative Philology at Oxford. Post 8vo. Cloth, price 9*s.*

Ginevra and The Duke of Guise. Two Tragedies. Crown 8vo. Cloth, price 6*s.*

GLOVER (F.), M.A.

Exempla Latina. A First Construing Book with Short Notes, Lexicon, and an Introduction to the Analysis of Sentences. Fcap. 8vo. Cloth, price 2*s.*

GODWIN (William).

William Godwin: His Friends and Contemporaries. With Portraits and Facsimiles of the handwriting of Godwin and his Wife. By C. Kegan Paul. 2 vols. Demy 8vo. Cloth, price 28*s.*

The Genius of Christianity Unveiled. Being Essays never before published. Edited, with a Preface, by C. Kegan Paul. Crown 8vo. Cloth, price 7*s.* 6*d.*

GOETZE (Capt. A. von).

Operations of the German Engineers during the War of 1870-1871. Published by Authority, and in accordance with Official Documents. Translated from the German by Colonel G. Graham, V.C., C.B., R.E. With 6 large Maps. Demy 8vo. Cloth, price 21*s.*

GOLDSMID (Sir Francis Henry).

Memoir of. With Portrait. Crown 8vo. Cloth, price 5*s.*

GOODENOUGH (Commodore J. G.), R.N., C.B., C.M.G.

Memoir of, with Extracts from his Letters and Journals. Edited by his Widow. With Steel Engraved Portrait. Square 8vo. Cloth, 5*s.*

*** Also a Library Edition with Maps, Woodcuts, and Steel Engraved Portrait. Square post 8vo. Cloth, price 14*s.*

GOSSE (Edmund W.).
Studies in the Literature of Northern Europe. With a Frontispiece designed and etched by Alma Tadema. Large post 8vo. Cloth, price 12*s*.

New Poems. Crown 8vo. Cloth, price 7*s*. 6*d*.

GOULD (Rev. S. Baring), M.A.
Germany, Present and Past. 2 Vols. Demy 8vo. Cloth, price 21*s*.

The Vicar of Morwenstow: a Memoir of the Rev. R. S. Hawker. With Portrait. Third Edition, revised. Square post 8vo. Cloth, 10*s*. 6*d*.

GREY (John), of Dilston.
John Grey (of Dilston): Memoirs. By Josephine E. Butler. New and Revised Edition. Crown 8vo. Cloth, price 3*s*. 6*d*.

GRIMLEY (Rev. H. N.), M.A.
Tremadoc Sermons, chiefly on the SPIRITUAL BODY, the UNSEEN WORLD, and the DIVINE HUMANITY. Second Edition. Crown 8vo. Cloth, price 6*s*.

GRÜNER (M. L.).
Studies of Blast Furnace Phenomena. Translated by L. D. B. Gordon, F.R.S.E., F.G.S. Demy 8vo. Cloth, price 7*s*. 6*d*.

GURNEY (Rev. Archer).
Words of Faith and Cheer. A Mission of Instruction and Suggestion. Crown 8vo. Cloth, price 6*s*.

Gwen: A Drama in Monologue. By the Author of the "Epic of Hades." Second Edition. Fcap. 8vo. Cloth, price 5*s*.

HAECKEL (Prof. Ernst).
The History of Creation. Translation revised by Professor E. Ray Lankester, M.A., F.R.S. With Coloured Plates and Genealogical Trees of the various groups of both plants and animals. 2 vols. Second Edition. Post 8vo. Cloth, price 32*s*.

The History of the Evolution of Man. With numerous Illustrations. 2 vols. Large post 8vo. Cloth, price 32*s*.

HAECKEL (Prof. Ernst.)—*continued.*
Freedom in Science and Teaching. From the German of Ernst Haeckel, with a Prefatory Note by T. H. Huxley, F.R.S. Crown 8vo. Cloth, price 5*s*.

HAKE (A. Egmont).
Paris Originals, with twenty etchings, by Léon Richeton. Large post 8vo. Cloth, price 14*s*.

Halleck's International Law; or, Rules Regulating the Intercourse of States in Peace and War. A New Edition, revised, with Notes and Cases. By Sir Sherston Baker, Bart. 2 vols. Demy 8vo. Cloth, price 38*s*.

HARDY (Thomas).
A Pair of Blue Eyes. New Edition. With Frontispiece. Crown 8vo. Cloth, price 6*s*.

The Return of the Native. New Edition. With Frontispiece. Crown 8vo. Cloth, price 6*s*.

HARRISON (Lieut.-Col. R.).
The Officer's Memorandum Book for Peace and War. Second Edition. Oblong 32mo. roan, elastic band and pencil, price 3*s*. 6*d*.; russia, 5*s*.

HARTINGTON (The Right Hon. the Marquis of), M.P.
Election Speeches in 1879 and 1880. With Address to the Electors of North-East Lancashire. Crown 8vo. Cloth, price 3*s*. 6*d*.

HAWEIS (Rev. H. R.), M.A.
Arrows in the Air. Crown 8vo. Second Edition. Cloth, price 6*s*.

Current Coin. Materialism—The Devil—Crime—Drunkenness—Pauperism—Emotion—Recreation—The Sabbath. Third Edition. Crown 8vo. Cloth, price 6*s*.

Speech in Season. Fourth Edition. Crown 8vo. Cloth, price 9*s*.

Thoughts for the Times. Eleventh Edition. Crown 8vo. Cloth, price 7*s*. 6*d*.

Unsectarian Family Prayers. New and Cheaper Edition. Fcap. 8vo. Cloth, price 1*s*. 6*d*.

HAWKER (Robert Stephen).
The Poetical Works of. Now first collected and arranged with a prefatory notice by J. G. Godwin. With Portrait. Crown 8vo. Cloth, price 12*s.*

HAWTREY (Edward M.).
Corydalis. A Story of the Sicilian Expedition. Small crown 8vo. Cloth, price 3*s.* 6*d.*

HEIDENHAIN (Rudolf), M.D.
Animal Magnetism. Physiological Observations. Translated from the Fourth German Edition, by L. C. Wooldridge. With a Preface by G. R. Romanes, F.R.S. Crown 8vo. Cloth, price 2*s.* 6*d.*

HELLWALD (Baron F. von).
The Russians in Central Asia. A Critical Examination, down to the present time, of the Geography and History of Central Asia. Translated by Lieut.-Col. Theodore Wirgman, LL.B. Large post 8vo. With Map. Cloth, price 12*s.*

HELVIG (Major H.).
The Operations of the Bavarian Army Corps. Translated by Captain G. S. Schwabe. With Five large Maps. In 2 vols. Demy 8vo. Cloth, price 24*s.*

Tactical Examples: Vol. I. The Battalion, price 15*s.* Vol. II. The Regiment and Brigade, price 10*s.* 6*d.* Translated from the German by Col. Sir Lumley Graham. With numerous Diagrams. Demy 8vo. Cloth.

HERFORD (Brooke).
The Story of Religion in England. A Book for Young Folk. Crown 8vo. Cloth, price 5*s.*

HINTON (James).
Life and Letters of. Edited by Ellice Hopkins, with an Introduction by Sir W. W. Gull, Bart., and Portrait engraved on Steel by C. H. Jeens. Second Edition. Crown 8vo. Cloth, 8*s.* 6*d.*

Chapters on the Art of Thinking, and other Essays. With an Introduction by Shadworth Hodgson. Edited by C. H. Hinton. Crown 8vo. Cloth, price 8*s.* 6*d.*

HINTON (James)—*continued.*
The Place of the Physician. To which is added ESSAYS ON THE LAW OF HUMAN LIFE, AND ON THE RELATION BETWEEN ORGANIC AND INORGANIC WORLDS. Second Edition. Crown 8vo. Cloth, price 3*s.* 6*d.*

Physiology for Practical Use. By various Writers. With 50 Illustrations. 2 vols. Second Edition. Crown 8vo. Cloth, price 12*s.* 6*d.*

An Atlas of Diseases of the Membrana Tympani. With Descriptive Text. Post 8vo. Price £6 6*s.*

The Questions of Aural Surgery. With Illustrations. 2 vols. Post 8vo. Cloth, price 12*s.* 6*d.*

The Mystery of Pain. New Edition. Fcap. 8vo. Cloth limp, 1*s.*

HOCKLEY (W. B.).
Tales of the Zenana; or, A Nuwab's Leisure Hours. By the Author of "Pandurang Hari." With a Preface by Lord Stanley of Alderley. 2 vols. Crown 8vo. Cloth, price 21*s.*

Pandurang Hari; or, Memoirs of a Hindoo. A Tale of Mahratta Life sixty years ago. With a Preface by Sir H. Bartle E. Frere, G.C.S.I., &c. New and Cheaper Edition. Crown 8vo. Cloth, price 6*s.*

HOFFBAUER (Capt.).
The German Artillery in the Battles near Metz. Based on the official reports of the German Artillery. Translated by Capt. E. O. Hollist. With Map and Plans. Demy 8vo. Cloth, price 21*s.*

HOLMES (E. G. A.).
Poems. First and Second Series. Fcap. 8vo. Cloth, price 5*s.* each.

HOLROYD (Major W. R. M.).
Tas-hil ul Kālām; or, Hindustani made Easy. Crown 8vo. Cloth, price 5*s.*

HOOPER (Mary).
Little Dinners: How to Serve them with Elegance and Economy. Thirteenth Edition. Crown 8vo. Cloth, price 5*s.*

HOOPER (Mary)—*continued.*

Cookery for Invalids, Persons of Delicate Digestion, and Children. Crown 8vo. Cloth, price 3*s.* 6*d.*

Every-Day Meals. Being Economical and Wholesome Recipes for Breakfast, Luncheon, and Supper. Second Edition. Crown 8vo. Cloth, price 5*s.*

HOOPER (Mrs. G.).

The House of Raby. With a Frontispiece. Crown 8vo. Cloth, price 3*s.* 6*d.*

HOPKINS (Ellice).

Life and Letters of James Hinton, with an Introduction by Sir W. W. Gull, Bart., and Portrait engraved on Steel by C. H. Jeens. Second Edition. Crown 8vo. Cloth price 8*s.* 6*d.*

HOPKINS (M.).

The Port of Refuge; or, Counsel and Aid to Shipmasters in Difficulty, Doubt, or Distress. Crown 8vo. Second and Revised Edition. Cloth, price 6*s.*

HORNER (The Misses).

Walks in Florence. A New and thoroughly Revised Edition. 2 vols. Crown 8vo. Cloth limp. With Illustrations.

Vol. I.—Churches, Streets, and Palaces. 10*s.* 6*d.* Vol. II.—Public Galleries and Museums. 5*s.*

HULL (Edmund C. P.).

The European in India. With a Medical Guide for Anglo-Indians. By R. R. S. Mair, M.D., F.R.C.S.E. Third Edition, Revised and Corrected. Post 8vo. Cloth, price 6*s.*

HUTCHISON (Lieut.-Col. F. J.), and Capt. G. H. MACGREGOR.

Military Sketching and Reconnaissance. With Fifteen Plates. Small 8vo. Cloth, price 6*s.*

The first Volume of Military Handbooks for Regimental Officers. Edited by Lieut.-Col. C. B. Brackenbury, R.A., A.A.G.

HUTTON (Arthur), M.A.

The Anglican Ministry. Its Nature and Value in relation to the Catholic Priesthood. With a Preface by his Eminence Cardinal Newman. Demy 8vo. Cloth, price 14*s.*

HUXLEY (Prof.)

The Crayfish: An Introduction to the Study of Zoology. With Eighty-two Illustrations. Crown 8vo. Cloth, price 5*s.*

Volume XXVIII. of the International Scientific Scientific Series.

INCHBOLD (J. W.).

Annus Amoris. Sonnets. Fcap. 8vo. Cloth, price 4*s.* 6*d.*

INGELOW (Jean).

Off the Skelligs. A Novel. With Frontispiece. Second Edition. Crown 8vo. Cloth, price 6*s.*

The Little Wonder-horn. A Second Series of "Stories Told to a Child." With Fifteen Illustrations. Small 8vo. Cloth, price 2*s.* 6*d.*

Indian Bishoprics. By an Indian Churchman. Demy 8vo. 6*d.*

International Scientific Series (The).

I. **Forms of Water: A Familiar Exposition of the Origin and Phenomena of Glaciers.** By J. Tyndall, LL.D., F.R.S. With 25 Illustrations. Seventh Edition. Crown 8vo. Cloth, price 5*s.*

II. **Physics and Politics**; or, Thoughts on the Application of the Principles of "Natural Selection" and "Inheritance" to Political Society. By Walter Bagehot. Fifth Edition. Crown 8vo. Cloth, price 4*s.*

III. **Foods.** By Edward Smith, M.D., &c. With numerous Illustrations. Sixth Edition. Crown 8vo. Cloth, price 5*s.*

IV. **Mind and Body:** The Theories of their Relation. By Alexander Bain, LL.D. With Four Illustrations. Seventh Edition. Crown 8vo. Cloth, price 4*s.*

V. **The Study of Sociology.** By Herbert Spencer. Eighth Edition. Crown 8vo. Cloth, price 5*s.*

International Scientific Series (The)—*continued.*

VI. On the Conservation of Energy. By Balfour Stewart, LL.D., &c. With 14 Illustrations. Fifth Edition. Crown 8vo. Cloth, price 5*s.*

VII. Animal Locomotion; or, Walking, Swimming, and Flying. By J. B. Pettigrew, M.D., &c. With 130 Illustrations. Second Edition. Crown 8vo. Cloth, price 5*s.*

VIII. Responsibility in Mental Disease. By Henry Maudsley, M.D. Third Edition. Crown 8vo. Cloth, price 5*s.*

IX. The New Chemistry. By Professor J. P. Cooke. With 31 Illustrations. Fifth Edition. Crown 8vo. Cloth, price 5*s.*

X. The Science of Law. By Prof. Sheldon Amos. Fourth Edition. Crown 8vo. Cloth, price 5*s.*

XI. Animal Mechanism. A Treatise on Terrestrial and Aerial Locomotion. By Prof. E. J. Marey. With 117 Illustrations. Second Edition. Crown 8vo. Cloth, price 5*s.*

XII. The Doctrine of Descent and Darwinism. By Prof. Osca Schmidt. With 26 Illustrations. Third Edition. Crown 8vo. Cloth, price 5*s.*

XIII. The History of the Conflict between Religion and Science. By J. W. Draper, M.D., LL.D. Fourteenth Edition. Crown 8vo. Cloth, price 5*s.*

XIV. Fungi; their Nature, Influences, Uses, &c. By M. C. Cooke, LL.D. Edited by the Rev. M. J. Berkeley, F.L.S. With numerous Illustrations. Second Edition. Crown 8vo. Cloth, price 5*s.*

XV. The Chemical Effects of Light and Photography. By Dr. Hermann Vogel. With 100 Illustrations. Third and Revised Edition. Crown 8vo. Cloth, price 5*s.*

XVI. The Life and Growth of Language. By Prof. William Dwight Whitney. Second Edition. Crown 8vo. Cloth, price 5*s.*

XVII. Money and the Mechanism of Exchange. By W. Stanley Jevons, F.R.S. Fourth Edition. Crown 8vo. Cloth, price 5*s.*

International Scientific Series (The)—*continued.*

XVIII. The Nature of Light: With a General Account of Physical Optics. By Dr. Eugene Lommel. With 188 Illustrations and a table of Spectra in Chromo-lithography. Third Edition. Crown 8vo. Cloth, price 5*s.*

XIX. Animal Parasites and Messmates. By M. Van Beneden. With 83 Illustrations. Second Edition. Crown 8vo. Cloth, price 5*s.*

XX. Fermentation. By Prof. Schützenberger. With 28 Illustrations. Second Edition. Crown 8vo. Cloth, price 5*s.*

XXI. The Five Senses of Man. By Prof. Bernstein. With 91 Illustrations. Second Edition. Crown 8vo. Cloth, price 5*s.*

XXII. The Theory of Sound in its Relation to Music. By Prof. Pietro Blaserna. With numerous Illustrations. Second Edition. Crown 8vo. Cloth, price 5*s.*

XXIII. Studies in Spectrum Analysis. By J. Norman Lockyer. F.R.S. With six photographic Illustrations of Spectra, and numerous engravings on wood. Crown 8vo. Second Edition. Cloth, price 6*s.* 6*d.*

XXIV. A History of the Growth of the Steam Engine. By Prof. R. H. Thurston. With numerous Illustrations. Second Edition. Crown 8vo. Cloth, price 6*s.* 6*d.*

XXV. Education as a Science. By Alexander Bain, LL.D. Third Edition. Crown 8vo. Cloth, price 5*s.*

XXVI. The Human Species. By Prof. A. de Quatrefages. Second Edition. Crown 8vo. Cloth, price 5*s.*

XXVII. Modern Chromatics. With Applications to Art and Industry, by Ogden N. Rood. With 130 original Illustrations. Crown 8vo. Cloth, price 5*s.*

XXVIII. The Crayfish: an Introduction to the Study of Zoology. By Prof. T. H. Huxley. With eighty-two Illustrations. Crown 8vo. Cloth, price 5*s.*

XXIX. The Brain as an Organ of Mind. By H. Charlton Bastian, M.D. With numerous Illustrations. Second Edition. Crown 8vo. Cloth, price 5*s.*

International Scientific Series (The)—*continued.*

Forthcoming Volumes.

Prof. W. KINGDON CLIFFORD, M.A. The First Principles of the Exact Sciences explained to the Non-mathematical.

W. B. CARPENTER, LL.D., F.R.S. The Physical Geography of the Sea.

Sir JOHN LUBBOCK, Bart., F.R.S. On Ants and Bees.

Prof. W. T. THISELTON DYER, B.A., B.Sc. Form and Habit in Flowering Plants.

Prof. MICHAEL FOSTER, M.D. Protoplasm and the Cell Theory.

Prof. A. C. RAMSAY, LL.D., F.R.S. Earth Sculpture: Hills, Valleys, Mountains, Plains, Rivers, Lakes; how they were Produced, and how they have been Destroyed.

P. BERT (Professor of Physiology, Paris). Forms of Life and other Cosmical Conditions.

The Rev. A SECCHI, D.J., late Director of the Observatory at Rome. The Stars.

Prof. J. ROSENTHAL, of the University of Erlangen. General Physiology of Muscles and Nerves.

FRANCIS GALTON, F.R.S. Psychometry.

J. W. JUDD, F.R.S. The Laws of Volcanic Action.

Prof. F. N. BALFOUR. The Embryonic Phases of Animal Life.

J. LUYS, Physician to the Hospice de la Salpétrière. The Brain and its Functions. With Illustrations.

Dr. CARL SEMPER. Animals and their Conditions of Existence.

Prof. WURTZ. Atoms and the Atomic Theory.

GEORGE J. ROMANES, F.L.S. Animal Intelligence.

ALFRED W. BENNETT. A Handbook of Cryptogamic Botany.

JENKINS (Rev. Canon).

The Girdle Legend of Prato. Small crown 8vo. Cloth, price 2*s.*

JENKINS (E.) and RAYMOND (J.), Esqs.

A Legal Handbook for Architects, Builders, and Building Owners. Second Edition Revised. Crown 8vo. Cloth, price 6*s.*

JENKINS (Rev. R. C.), M.A.

The Privilege of Peter and the Claims of the Roman Church confronted with the Scriptures, the Councils, and the Testimony of the Popes themselves. Fcap. 8vo. Cloth, price 3*s.* 6*d.*

JENNINGS (Mrs. Vaughan).

Rahel: Her Life and Letters. With a Portrait from the Painting by Daffinger. Square post 8vo. Cloth, price 7*s.* 6*d.*

Jeroveam's Wife and other Poems. Fcap. 8vo. Cloth, price 3*s.* 6*d.*

JEVONS (W. Stanley), M.A., F.R.S.

Money and the Mechanism of Exchange. Fourth Edition. Crown 8vo. Cloth, price 5*s.*

Volume XVII. of The International Scientific Series.

JOEL (L.).

A Consul's Manual and Shipowner's and Shipmaster's Practical Guide in their Transactions Abroad. With Definitions of Nautical, Mercantile, and Legal Terms; a Glossary of Mercantile Terms in English, French, German, Italian, and Spanish. Tables of the Money, Weights, and Measures of the Principal Commercial Nations and their Equivalents in British Standards; and Forms of Consular and Notarial Acts. Demy 8vo. Cloth, price 12*s.*

JOHNSTONE (C. F.), M.A.

Historical Abstracts. Being Outlines of the History of some of the less-known States of Europe. Crown 8vo. Cloth, price 7*s.* 6*d.*

JONES (Lucy).

Puddings and Sweets. Being Three Hundred and Sixty-Five Receipts approved by Experience. Crown 8vo., price 2*s.* 6*d.*

JOYCE (P. W.), LL.D., &c.
Old Celtic Romances. Translated from the Gaelic by. Crown 8vo. Cloth, price 7*s.* 6*d.*

KAUFMANN (Rev. M.), B.A.
Utopias; or, Schemes of Social Improvement, from Sir Thomas More to Karl Marx. Crown 8vo. Cloth, price 5*s.*

Socialism: Its Nature, its Dangers, and its Remedies considered. Crown 8vo. Cloth, price 7*s.* 6*d.*

KAY (Joseph), M.A., Q.C.
Free Trade in Land. Edited by his Widow. With Preface by the Right Hon. John Bright, M.P. Third Edition. Crown 8vo. Cloth, price 5*s.*

KENT (Carolo).
Carona Catholica ad Petri successoris Pedes Oblata. De Summi Pontificis Leonis XIII. Assumptione Epiggramma. In Quinquaginta Linguis. Fcap. 4to. Cloth, price 15*s.*

KER (David).
The Boy Slave in Bokhara. A Tale of Central Asia. With Illustrations. Crown 8vo. Cloth, price 3*s.* 6*d.*

The Wild Horseman of the Pampas. Illustrated. Crown 8vo. Cloth, price 3*s.* 6*d.*

KERNER (Dr. A.), Professor of Botany in the University of Innsbruck.
Flowers and their Unbidden Guests. Translation edited by W. OGLE, M.A., M.D., and a prefatory letter by C. Darwin, F.R.S. With Illustrations. Sq. 8vo. Cloth, price 9*s.*

KIDD (Joseph), M.D.
The Laws of Therapeutics, or, the Science and Art of Medicine. Crown 8vo. Cloth, price 6*s.*

KINAHAN (G. Henry), M.R.I.A., &c., of her Majesty's Geological Survey.
Manual of the Geology of Ireland. With 8 Plates, 26 Woodcuts, and a Map of Ireland, geologically coloured. Square 8vo. Cloth, price 15*s.*

KING (Mrs. Hamilton).
The Disciples. A Poem. Third Edition, with some Notes. Crown 8vo. Cloth, price 7*s.* 6*d.*

Aspromonte, and other Poems. Second Edition. Fcap. 8vo. Cloth, price 4*s.* 6*d.*

KING (Edward).
Echoes from the Orient. With Miscellaneous Poems. Small crown 8vo. Cloth, price 3*s.* 6*d.*

KINGSLEY (Charles), M.A.
Letters and Memories of his Life. Edited by his WIFE. With 2 Steel engraved Portraits and numerous Illustrations on Wood, and a Facsimile of his Handwriting. Thirteenth Edition. 2 vols. Demy 8vo. Cloth, price 36*s.*

*** Also a Cabinet Edition in 2 vols. Crown 8vo. Cloth, price 12*s.*

All Saints' Day and other Sermons. Second Edition. Crown 8vo. Cloth, 7*s.* 6*d.*

True Words for Brave Men: a Book for Soldiers' and Sailors' Libraries. Fifth Edition. Crown 8vo. Cloth, price 2*s.* 6*d.*

KNIGHT (Professor W.).
Studies in Philosophy and Literature. Large post 8vo. Cloth, price 7*s.* 6*d.*

LACORDAIRE (Rev. Père).
Life: Conferences delivered at Toulouse. A New and Cheaper Edition. Crown 8vo. Cloth, price 3*s.* 6*d.*

LAIRD-CLOWES (W.).
Love's Rebellion: a Poem. Fcap. 8vo. Cloth, price 3*s.* 6*d.*

LAMONT (Martha MacDonald).
The Gladiator: A Life under the Roman Empire in the beginning of the Third Century. With four Illustrations by H. M. Paget. Extra fcap. 8vo. Cloth, price 3*s.* 6*d.*

LANG (A.).
XXII Ballades in Blue China. Elzevir. 8vo. Parchment, price 3*s.* 6*d.*

LAYMANN (Capt.).
The Frontal Attack of Infantry. Translated by Colonel Edward Newdigate. Crown 8vo. Cloth, price 2*s.* 6*d.*

LEANDER (Richard).
Fantastic Stories. Translated from the German by Paulina B. Granville. With Eight full-page Illustrations by M. E. Fraser-Tytler. Crown 8vo. Cloth, price 5*s*.

LEE (Rev. F. G.), D.C.L.
The Other World; or, Glimpses of the Supernatural. 2 vols. A New Edition. Crown 8vo. Cloth, price 15*s*.

LEE (Holme).
Her Title of Honour. A Book for Girls. New Edition. With a Frontispiece. Crown 8vo. Cloth, price 5*s*.

LEWIS (Edward Dillon).
A Draft Code of Criminal Law and Procedure. Demy 8vo. Cloth, price 21*s*.

LEWIS (Mary A.).
A Rat with Three Tales. With Four Illustrations by Catherine F. Frere. Crown 8vo. Cloth, price 5*s*.

LINDSAY (W. Lauder), M.D., &c.
Mind in the Lower Animals in Health and Disease. 2 vols. Demy 8vo. Cloth, price 32*s*.

LLOYD (Francis) and Charles Tebbitt.
Extension of Empire Weakness? Deficits Ruin? With a Practical Scheme for the Reconstruction of Asiatic Turkey. Small crown 8vo. Cloth, price 3*s*. 6*d*.

LOCKER (F.).
London Lyrics. A New and Revised Edition, with Additions and a Portrait of the Author. Crown 8vo. Cloth, elegant, price 6*s*.
Also, a Cheaper Edition. Fcap 8vo. Cloth, price 2*s*. 6*d*.

LOCKYER (J. Norman), F.R.S.
Studies in Spectrum Analysis; with six photographic illustrations of Spectra, and numerous engravings on wood. Second Edition. Crown 8vo. Cloth, price 6*s*. 6*d*.
Vol. XXIII. of The International Scientific Series.

LOMMEL (Dr. E.).
The Nature of Light: With a General Account of Physical Optics. Second Edition. With 188 Illustrations and a Table of Spectra in Chromo-lithography. Third Edition. Crown 8vo. Cloth, price 5*s*.
Volume XVIII. of The International Scientific Series.

LONSDALE (Margaret).
Sister Dora. A Biography, with Portrait engraved on steel by C. H. Jeens, and one illustration. Twelfth edition. Crown 8vo. Cloth, price 6*s*.

LORIMER (Peter), D.D.
John Knox and the Church of England: His Work in her Pulpit, and his Influence upon her Liturgy, Articles, and Parties. Demy 8vo. Cloth, price 12*s*.

John Wiclif and his English Precursors, by Gerhard Victor Lechler. Translated from the German, with additional Notes. 2 vols. Demy 8vo. Cloth, price 21*s*.

Love's Gamut and other Poems. Small crown 8vo. Cloth, price 3*s*. 6*d*.

LOWNDES (Henry).
Poems and Translations. Crown 8vo. Cloth, price 6*s*.

MAC CLINTOCK (L.).
Sir Spangle and the Dingy Hen. Illustrated. Square crown 8vo., price 2*s*. 6*d*.

MACDONALD (G.).
Malcolm. With Portrait of the Author engraved on Steel. Fourth Edition. Crown 8vo. Price 6*s*.

The Marquis of Lossie. Second Edition. Crown 8vo. Cloth, price 6*s*.

St. George and St. Michael. Second Edition. Crown 8vo. Cloth, 6*s*.

MACKENNA (S. J.).
Plucky Fellows. A Book for Boys. With Six Illustrations. Fourth Edition. Crown 8vo. Cloth, price 3*s*. 6*d*.

At School with an Old Dragoon. With Six Illustrations. Second Edition. Crown 8vo. Cloth, price 5*s*.

MACLACHLAN (Mrs.).

Notes and Extracts on Everlasting Punishment and Eternal Life, according to Literal Interpretation. Small crown 8vo. Cloth, price 3*s*. 6*d*.

MACNAUGHT (Rev. John).

Cœna Domini: An Essay on the Lord's Supper, its Primitive Institution, Apostolic Uses, and Subsequent History. Demy 8vo. Cloth, price 14*s*.

MAGNUSSON (Eirikr), M.A., and **PALMER** (E.H.), M.A.

Johan Ludvig Runeberg's Lyrical Songs, Idylls and Epigrams. Fcap. 8vo. Cloth, price 5*s*.

MAIR (R. S.), M.D., F.R.C.S.E.

The Medical Guide for Anglo-Indians. Being a Compendium of Advice to Europeans in India, relating to the Preservation and Regulation of Health. With a Supplement on the Management of Children in India. Second Edition. Crown 8vo. Limp cloth, price 3*s*. 6*d*.

MALDEN (H. E. and E. E.)

Princes and Princesses. Illustrated. Small crown 8vo. Cloth, price 2*s*. 6*d*.

MANNING (His Eminence Cardinal).

Essays on Religion and Literature. By various Writers. Third Series. Demy 8vo. Cloth, price 10*s*. 6*d*.

The Independence of the Holy See, with an Appendix containing the Papal Allocution and a translation. Cr. 8vo. Cloth, price 5*s*.

The True Story of the Vatican Council. Crown 8vo. Cloth, price 5*s*.

MAREY (E. J.).

Animal Mechanics. A Treatise on Terrestrial and Aerial Locomotion. With 117 Illustrations. Second Edition. Crown 8vo. Cloth, price 5*s*.

Volume XI. of The International Scientific Series.

MARKHAM (Capt. Albert Hastings), R.N.

The Great Frozen Sea. A Personal Narrative of the Voyage of the "Alert" during the Arctic Expedition of 1875-6. With six full-page Illustrations, two Maps, and twenty-seven Woodcuts. Fourth and cheaper edition. Crown 8vo. Cloth, price 6*s*.

Master Bobby: a Tale. By the Author of "Christina North." With Illustrations by E. H. Bell. Extra fcap. 8vo. Cloth, price 3*s*.6*d*.

MASTERMAN (J.).

Half-a-dozen Daughters. With a Frontispiece. Crown 8vo. Cloth, price 3*s*. 6*d*.

MAUDSLEY (Dr. H.).

Responsibility in Mental Disease. Third Edition. Crown 8vo. Cloth, price 5*s*.

Volume VIII. of The International Scientific Series.

MEREDITH (George).

The Egoist. A Comedy in Narrative. 3 vols. Crown 8vo. Cloth.

*** Also a Cheaper Edition, with Frontispiece. Crown 8vo. Cloth, price 6*s*.

The Ordeal of Richard Feverel. A History of Father and Son. In one vol. with Frontispiece. Crown 8vo. Cloth, price 6*s*.

MERRITT (Henry).

Art - Criticism and Romance. With Recollections, and Twenty-three Illustrations in *eau-forte*, by Anna Lea Merritt. Two vols. Large post 8vo. Cloth, 25*s*.

MIDDLETON (The Lady).

Ballads. Square 16mo. Cloth, price 3*s*. 6*d*.

MILLER (Edward).

The History and Doctrines of Irvingism; or, the so-called Catholic and Apostolic Church. 2 vols. Large post 8vo. Cloth, price 25*s*.

The Church in Relation to the State. Crown 8vo. Cloth, price 7*s*. 6*d*.

MILNE (James).
Tables of Exchange for the Conversion of Sterling Money into Indian and Ceylon Currency, at Rates from 1*s*. 8*d*. to 2*s*. 3*d*. per Rupee. Second Edition. Demy 8vo. Cloth, price £2 2*s*.

MINCHIN (J. G.).
Bulgaria since the War. Notes of a Tour in the Autumn of 1879. Small crown 8vo. Cloth, price 3*s*. 6*d*.

MIVART (St. George), F.R.S.
Contemporary Evolution: An Essay on some recent Social Changes. Post 8vo. Cloth, price 7*s*. 6*d*.

MOCKLER (E.).
A Grammar of the Baloochee Language, as it is spoken in Makran (Ancient Gedrosia), in the Persia-Arabic and Roman characters. Fcap. 8vo. Cloth, price 5*s*.

MOFFAT (Robert Scott).
The Economy of Consumption; an Omitted Chapter in Political Economy, with special reference to the Questions of Commercial Crises and the Policy of Trades Unions; and with Reviews of the Theories of Adam Smith, Ricardo, J. S. Mill, Fawcett, &c. Demy 8vo. Cloth, price 18*s*.

The Principles of a Time Policy: being an Exposition of a Method of Settling Disputes between Employers and Employed in regard to Time and Wages, by a simple Process of Mercantile Barter, without recourse to Strikes or Locks-out. Reprinted from "The Economy of Consumption," with a Preface and Appendix containing Observations on some Reviews of that book, and a Recriticism of the Theories of Ricardo and J. S. Mill on Rent, Value, and Cost of Production. Demy 8vo. Cloth, price 3*s*. 6*d*.

MOLTKE (Field-Marshal Von).
Letters from Russia. Translated by Robina Napier. Crown 8vo. Cloth, price 6*s*.

Notes of Travel. Being Extracts from the Journals of. Crown 8vo. Cloth, price 6*s*.

Monmouth: A Drama, of which the Outline is Historical. Dedicated by permission to Mr. Henry Irving. Small crown 8vo. Cloth, price 5*s*.

MORELL (J. R.).
Euclid Simplified in Method and Language. Being a Manual of Geometry. Compiled from the most important French Works, approved by the University of Paris and the Minister of Public Instruction. Fcap. 8vo. Cloth, price 2*s*. 6*d*.

MORICE (Rev. F. D.), M.A.
The Olympian and Pythian Odes of Pindar. A New Translation in English Verse. Crown 8vo. Cloth, price 7*s*. 6*d*.

MORSE (E. S.), Ph.D.
First Book of Zoology. With numerous Illustrations. Crown 8vo. Cloth, price 5*s*.

MORSHEAD (E. D. A.)
The Agamemnon of Æschylus. Translated into English verse. With an Introductory Essay. Crown 8vo. Cloth, price 5*s*.

MORTERRA (Felix).
The Legend of Allandale, and other Poems. Small crown 8vo. Cloth, price 6*s*.

NAAKE (J. T.).
Slavonic Fairy Tales. From Russian, Servian, Polish, and Bohemian Sources. With Four Illustrations. Crown 8vo. Cloth, price 5*s*.

NEWMAN (J. H.), D.D.
Characteristics from the Writings of. Being Selections from his various Works. Arranged with the Author's personal approval. Third Edition. With Portrait. Crown 8vo. Cloth, price 6*s*.

*** A Portrait of the Rev. Dr. J. H. Newman, mounted for framing, can be had, price 2*s*. 6*d*.

NICHOLAS (Thomas), Ph.D., F.G.S.
The Pedigree of the English People: an Argument, Historical and Scientific, on the Formation and Growth of the Nation, tracing Race-admixture in Britain from the earliest times, with especial reference to the incorporation of the Celtic Aborigines. Fifth Edition. Demy 8vo. Cloth, price 16*s*.

NICHOLSON (Edward Byron).

The Christ Child, and other Poems. Crown 8vo. Cloth, price 4*s*. 6*d*.

The Rights of an Animal. Crown 8vo. Cloth, price 3*s*. 6*d*.

The Gospel according to the Hebrews. Its Fragments translated and annotated, with a critical Analysis of the External and Internal Evidence relating to it. Demy 8vo. Cloth, price 9*s*. 6*d*.

NICOLS (Arthur), F.G.S., F.R.G.S.

Chapters from the Physical History of the Earth. An Introduction to Geology and Palæontology, with numerous illustrations. Crown 8vo. Cloth, price 5*s*.

NOAKE (Major R. Compton).

The Bivouac; or, Martial Lyrist, with an Appendix—Advice to the Soldier. Fcap. 8vo. Price 5*s*. 6*d*.

NORMAN PEOPLE (The).

The Norman People, and their Existing Descendants in the British Dominions and the United States of America. Demy 8vo. Cloth, price 21*s*.

NORRIS (Rev. Alfred).

The Inner and Outer Life Poems. Fcap. 8vo. Cloth, price 6*s*.

Notes on Cavalry Tactics, Organization, &c. By a Cavalry Officer. With Diagrams. Demy 8vo. Cloth, price 12*s*.

Nuces: Exercises on the Syntax of the Public School Latin Primer. New Edition in Three Parts. Crown 8vo. Each 1*s*.

*** The Three Parts can also be had bound together in cloth, price 3*s*.

O'BRIEN (Charlotte G.).

Light and Shade. 2 vols. Crown 8vo. Cloth, gilt tops, price 12*s*.

Ode of Life (The).

Third Edition. Fcap. 8vo. Cloth, price 5*s*.

O'HAGAN (John).

The Song of Roland. Translated into English Verse. Large post 8vo. Parchment antique, price 10*s*. 6*d*.

O'MEARA (Kathleen).

Frederic Ozanam, Professor of the Sorbonne; His Life and Works. Second Edition. Crown 8vo. Cloth, price 7*s*. 6*d*.

Oriental Sporting Magazine (The).

A Reprint of the first 5 Volumes, in 2 Volumes. Demy 8vo. Cloth, price 28*s*.

OWEN (F. M.).

John Keats. A Study. Crown 8vo. Cloth, price 6*s*.

OWEN (Rev. Robert), B.D.

Sanctorale Catholicum; or Book of Saints. With Notes, Critical, Exegetical, and Historical. Demy 8vo. Cloth, price 18*s*.

Palace and Prison and Fair Geraldine. Two Tragedies, by the Author of "Ginevra" and the "Duke of Guise." Crown 8vo. Cloth, 6*s*.

PALGRAVE (W. Gifford).

Hermann Agha; An Eastern Narrative. Third and Cheaper Edition. Crown 8vo. Cloth, price 6*s*.

PALMER (Charles Walter).

The Weed: a Poem. Small crown 8vo. Cloth, price 3*s*.

PANDURANG HARI;

Or, Memoirs of a Hindoo. With an Introductory Preface by Sir H. Bartle E. Frere, G.C.S.I., C.B. Crown 8vo. Price 6*s*.

PARKER (Joseph), D.D.

The Paraclete: An Essay on the Personality and Ministry of the Holy Ghost, with some reference to current discussions. Second Edition. Demy 8vo. Cloth, price 12*s*.

PARR (Capt. H. Hallam).

A Sketch of the Kafir and Zulu Wars: Guadana to Isandhlwana, with Maps. Small crown 8vo. Cloth, price 5*s*.

PARSLOE (Joseph).

Our Railways: Sketches, Historical and Descriptive. With Practical Information as to Fares, Rates, &c., and a Chapter on Railway Reform. Crown 8vo. Cloth, price 6*s*.

PATTISON (Mrs. Mark).

The Renaissance of Art in France. With Nineteen Steel Engravings. 2 vols. Demy 8vo. Cloth, price 32*s*.

PAUL (C. Kegan).

Mary Wollstonecraft. Letters to Imlay. With Prefatory Memoir by, and Two Portraits in *eau forte*, by Anna Lea Merritt. Crown 8vo. Cloth, price 6*s*.

Goethe's Faust. A New Translation in Rime. Crown 8vo. Cloth, price 6*s*.

William Godwin: His Friends and Contemporaries. With Portraits and Facsimiles of the Handwriting of Godwin and his Wife. 2 vols. Square post 8vo. Cloth, price 28*s*.

The Genius of Christianity Unveiled. Being Essays by William Godwin never before published. Edited, with a Preface, by C. Kegan Paul. Crown 8vo. Cloth, price 7*s*. 6*d*.

PAUL (Margaret Agnes).

Gentle and Simple: A Story. 2 vols. Crown 8vo. Cloth, gilt tops, price 12*s*.

*** Also a Cheaper Edition in one vol. with Frontispiece. Crown 8vo. Cloth, price 6*s*.

PAYNE (John).

Songs of Life and Death. Crown 8vo. Cloth, price 5*s*.

PAYNE (Prof. J. F.).

Lectures on Education. Price 6*d*.

II. Fröbel and the Kindergarten system. Second Edition.

PAYNE (Prof. J. F.)—*continued*.

A Visit to German Schools: Elementary Schools in Germany. Notes of a Professional Tour to inspect some of the Kindergartens, Primary Schools, Public Girls' Schools, and Schools for Technical Instruction in Hamburgh, Berlin, Dresden, Weimar, Gotha, Eisenach, in the autumn of 1874. With Critical Discussions of the General Principles and Practice of Kindergartens and other Schemes of Elementary Education. Crown 8vo. Cloth, price 4*s*. 6*d*.

PELLETAN (E.).

The Desert Pastor, Jean Jarousseau. Translated from the French. By Colonel E. P. De L'Hoste. With a Frontispiece. New Edition. Fcap. 8vo. Cloth, price 3*s*. 6*d*.

PENNELL (H. Cholmondeley).

Pegasus Resaddled. By the Author of "Puck on Pegasus," &c. &c. With Ten Full-page Illustrations by George Du Maurier. Second Edition. Fcap. 4to. Cloth elegant, price 12*s*. 6*d*.

PENRICE (Maj. J.), B.A.

A Dictionary and Glossary of the **Ko-ran.** With copious Grammatical References and Explanations of the Text. 4to. Cloth, price 21*s*.

PESCHEL (Dr. Oscar).

The Races of Man and their Geographical Distribution. Large crown 8vo. Cloth, price 9*s*.

PETTIGREW (J. Bell), M.D., F.R.S.

Animal Locomotion; or, Walking, Swimming, and Flying. With 130 Illustrations. Second Edition. Crown 8vo. Cloth, price 5*s*.

Volume VII. of The International Scientific Series.

PFEIFFER (Emily).

Quarterman's Grace, and other Poems. Crown 8vo. Cloth, price 5*s*.

Glan Alarch: His Silence and Song. A Poem. Second Edition. Crown 8vo. price 6*s*.

PFEIFFER (Emily)—*continued*.

Gerard's Monument, and other Poems. Second Edition. Crown 8vo. Cloth, price 6*s*.

Poems. Second Edition. Crown 8vo. Cloth, price 6*s*.

Sonnets and Songs. New Edition. 16mo, handsomely printed and bound in cloth, gilt edges, price 5*s*.

PINCHES (Thomas), M.A.

Samuel Wilberforce: Faith—Service—Recompense. Three Sermons. With a Portrait of Bishop Wilberforce (after a Photograph by Charles Watkins). Crown 8vo. Cloth, price 4*s*. 6*d*.

PLAYFAIR (Lieut.-Col.), Her Britannic Majesty's Consul-General in Algiers.

Travels in the Footsteps of Bruce in Algeria and Tunis. Illustrated by facsimiles of Bruce's original Drawings, Photographs, Maps, &c. Royal 4to. Cloth, bevelled boards, gilt leaves, price £3 3*s*.

POLLOCK (W. H.).

Lectures on French Poets. Delivered at the Royal Institution. Small crown 8vo. Cloth, price 5*s*.

POUSHKIN (A. S.).

Russian Romance. Translated from the Tales of Belkin, &c. By Mrs. J. Buchan Telfer (*née* Mouravieff). Crown 8vo. Cloth, price 3*s*. 6*d*.

PRESBYTER.

Unfoldings of Christian Hope. An Essay showing that the Doctrine contained in the Damnatory Clauses of the Creed commonly called Athanasian is unscriptural. Small crown 8vo. Cloth, price 4*s*. 6*d*.

PRICE (Prof. Bonamy).

Currency and Banking. Crown 8vo. Cloth, price 6*s*.

Chapters on Practical Political Economy. Being the Substance of Lectures delivered before the University of Oxford. Large post 8vo. Cloth, price 12*s*.

Proteus and Amadeus. A Correspondence. Edited by Aubrey De Vere. Crown 8vo. Cloth, price 5*s*.

PUBLIC SCHOOLBOY.

The Volunteer, the Militiaman, and the Regular Soldier. Crown 8vo. Cloth, price 5*s*.

PULPIT COMMENTARY (The).
Edited by the Rev. J. S. Exell and the Rev. Canon H. D. M. Spence.

Ezra, Nehemiah, and Esther. By Rev. Canon G. Rawlinson, M.A.; with Homilies by Rev. Prof. J. R. Thomson, M.A., Rev. Prof. R. A. Redford, LL.B., M.A., Rev. W. S. Lewis, M.A., Rev. J. A. Macdonald, Rev. A. Mackennal, B.A., Rev. W. Clarkson, B.A., Rev. F. Hastings, Rev. W. Dinwiddie, LL.B., Rev. Prof. Rowlands, B.A., Rev. G. Wood, B.A., Rev. Prof. P. C. Barker, LL.B., M.A., and Rev. J. S. Exell. Second Edition. One Vol., price 12*s*. 6*d*.

Punjaub (The) and North Western Frontier of India. By an old Punjaubee. Crown 8vo. Cloth, price 5*s*.

QUATREFAGES (Prof. A. de).

The Human Species. Second Edition. Crown 8vo. Cloth, price 5*s*.

Vol. XXVI. of The International Scientific Series.

RAVENSHAW (John Henry), B.C.S.

Gaur: Its Ruins and Inscriptions. Edited with considerable additions and alterations by his Widow. With forty-four photographic illustrations and twenty-five fac-similes of Inscriptions. Super royal 4to. Cloth, 3*l*. 13*s*. 6*d*.

READ (Carveth).

On the Theory of Logic: An Essay. Crown 8vo. Cloth, price 6*s*.

Realities of the Future Life. Small crown 8vo. Cloth, price 1*s*. 6*d*.

REANEY (Mrs. G. S.).

Blessing and Blessed; a Sketch of Girl Life. With a frontispiece. Crown 8vo. Cloth, price 5*s*.

Waking and Working; or, from Girlhood to Womanhood. With a Frontispiece. Crown 8vo. Cloth, price 5*s*.

English Girls: their Place and Power. With a Preface by R. W. Dale, M.A., of Birmingham. Second Edition. Fcap. 8vo. Cloth, price 2*s*. 6*d*.

Just Anyone, and other Stories. Three Illustrations. Royal 16mo. Cloth, price 1*s*. 6*d*.

Sunshine Jenny and other Stories. Three Illustrations. Royal 16mo. Cloth, price 1*s*. 6*d*.

Sunbeam Willie, and other Stories. Three Illustrations. Royal 16mo. Cloth, price 1*s*. 6*d*.

REYNOLDS (Rev. J. W.).

The Supernatural in Nature. A Verification by Free Use of Science. Second Edition, revised and enlarged. Demy 8vo. Cloth, price 14*s*.

Mystery of Miracles, The. By the Author of "The Supernatural in Nature." Crown 8vo. Cloth, price 6*s*.

RIBOT (Prof. Th.).

English Psychology. Second Edition. A Revised and Corrected Translation from the latest French Edition. Large post 8vo. Cloth, price 9*s*.

Heredity: A Psychological Study on its Phenomena, its Laws, its Causes, and its Consequences. Large crown 8vo. Cloth, price 9*s*.

RINK (Chevalier Dr. Henry).

Greenland: Its People and its Products. By the Chevalier Dr. HENRY RINK, President of the Greenland Board of Trade. With sixteen Illustrations, drawn by the Eskimo, and a Map. Edited by Dr. ROBERT BROWN. Crown 8vo. Price 10*s*. 6*d*.

ROBERTSON (The Late Rev. F. W.), M.A., of Brighton.

Notes on Genesis. New and cheaper Edition. Crown 8vo., price 3*s*. 6*d*.

Sermons. Four Series. Small crown 8vo. Cloth, price 3*s*. 6*d*. each.

Expository Lectures on St. Paul's Epistles to the Corinthians. A New Edition. Small crown 8vo. Cloth, price 5*s*.

Lectures and Addresses, with other literary remains. A New Edition. Crown 8vo. Cloth, price 5*s*.

An Analysis of Mr. Tennyson's "In Memoriam." (Dedicated by Permission to the Poet-Laureate.) Fcap. 8vo. Cloth, price 2*s*.

The Education of the Human Race. Translated from the German of Gotthold Ephraim Lessing. Fcap. 8vo. Cloth, price 2*s*. 6*d*.

Life and Letters. Edited by the Rev. Stopford Brooke, M.A., Chaplain in Ordinary to the Queen.

I. 2 vols., uniform with the Sermons. With Steel Portrait. Crown 8vo. Cloth, price 7*s*. 6*d*.

II. Library Edition, in Demy 8vo., with Two Steel Portraits. Cloth, price 12*s*.

III. A Popular Edition, in one vol. Crown 8vo. Cloth, price 6*s*.

The above Works can also be had half-bound in morocco.

*** A Portrait of the late Rev. F. W. Robertson, mounted for framing, can be had, price 2*s*. 6*d*.

ROBINSON (A. Mary F.).

A Handful of Honeysuckle. Fcap. 8vo. Cloth, price 3*s*. 6*d*.

RODWELL (G. F.), F.R.A.S., F.C.S.

Etna: a History of the Mountain and its Eruptions. With Maps and Illustrations. Square 8vo. Cloth, price 9*s*.

ROOD (Ogden N.).
Modern Chromatics, with Applications to Art and Industry. With 130 Original Illustrations. Crown 8vo. Cloth, price 5*s.*
Vol. XXVII. of The International Scientific Series.

ROSS (Mrs. E.), ("Nelsie Brook").
Daddy's Pet. A Sketch from Humble Life. With Six Illustrations. Royal 16mo. Cloth, price 1*s.*

ROSS (Alexander), D.D.
Memoir of Alexander Ewing, Bishop of Argyll and the Isles. Second and Cheaper Edition. Demy 8vo. Cloth, price 10*s.* 6*d.*

SADLER (S. W.), R.N.
The African Cruiser. A Midshipman's Adventures on the West Coast. With Three Illustrations. Second Edition. Crown 8vo. Cloth, price 3*s.* 6*d.*

SALTS (Rev. Alfred), LL.D.
Godparents at Confirmation. With a Preface by the Bishop of Manchester. Small crown 8vo. Cloth, limp, price 2*s.*

SAUNDERS (Katherine).
Gideon's Rock, and other Stories. Crown 8vo. Cloth, price 6*s.*
Joan Merryweather, and other Stories. Crown 8vo. Cloth, price 6*s.*
Margaret and Elizabeth. A Story of the Sea. Crown 8vo. Cloth, price 6*s.*

SAUNDERS (John).
Israel Mort, Overman: A Story of the Mine. Cr. 8vo. Price 6*s.*
Hirell. With Frontispiece. Crown 8vo. Cloth, price 3*s.* 6*d.*
Abel Drake's Wife. With Frontispiece. Crown 8vo. Cloth, price 3*s.* 6*d.*

SAYCE (Rev. Archibald Henry).
Introduction to the Science of Language. Two vols., large post 8vo. Cloth, price 25*s.*

SCHELL (Maj. von).
The Operations of the First Army under Gen. von Goeben. Translated by Col. C. H. von Wright. Four Maps. Demy 8vo. Cloth, price 9*s.*

SCHELL (Maj. von)—*continued.*
The Operations of the First Army under Gen. von Steinmetz. Translated by Captain E. O. Hollist. Demy 8vo. Cloth, price 10*s.* 6*d.*

SCHELLENDORF (Maj.-Gen. B. von).
The Duties of the General Staff. Translated from the German by Lieutenant Hare. Vol. I. Demy 8vo. Cloth, 10*s.* 6*d.*

SCHERFF (Maj. W. von).
Studies in the New Infantry Tactics. Parts I. and II. Translated from the German by Colonel Lumley Graham. Demy 8vo. Cloth, price 7*s.* 6*d.*

SCHMIDT (Prof. Oscar).
The Doctrine of Descent and Darwinism. With 26 Illustrations. Third Edition. Crown 8vo. Cloth, price 5*s.*
Volume XII. of The International Scientific Series.

SCHÜTZENBERGER (Prof. F.).
Fermentation. With Numerous Illustrations. Second Edition. Crown 8vo. Cloth, price 5*s.*
Volume XX. of The International Scientific Series.

SCOONES (W. Baptiste).
Four Centuries of English Letters. A Selection of 350 Letters by 150 Writers from the period of the Paston Letters to the Present Time. Edited and arranged by. Large crown 8vo. Cloth, price 9*s.*

SCOTT (Leader).
A Nook in the Apennines: A Summer beneath the Chestnuts. With Frontispiece, and 27 Illustrations in the Text, chiefly from Original Sketches. Crown 8vo. Cloth, price 7*s.* 6*d.*

SCOTT (Robert H.).
Weather Charts and Storm Warnings. Illustrated. Second Edition. Crown 8vo. Cloth, price 3*s.* 6*d.*

Seeking his Fortune, and other Stories. With Four Illustrations. Crown 8vo. Cloth, price 3*s.* 6*d.*

SENIOR (N. W.).

Alexis De Tocqueville. Correspondence and Conversations with Nassau W. Senior, from 1833 to 1859. Edited by M. C. M. Simpson. 2 vols. Large post 8vo. Cloth, price 21*s*.

Sermons to Naval Cadets.

Preached on board H.M.S. "Britannia." Small crown 8vo. Cloth, price 3*s*. 6*d*.

Seven Autumn Leaves from Fairyland. Illustrated with Nine Etchings. Square crown 8vo. Cloth, price 3*s*. 6*d*.

SHADWELL (Maj.-Gen.), C.B.

Mountain Warfare. Illustrated by the Campaign of 1799 in Switzerland. Being a Translation of the Swiss Narrative compiled from the Works of the Archduke Charles, Jomini, and others. Also of Notes by General H. Dufour on the Campaign of the Valtelline in 1635. With Appendix, Maps, and Introductory Remarks. Demy 8vo. Cloth, price 16*s*.

SHAKSPEARE (Charles).

Saint Paul at Athens: Spiritual Christianity in Relation to some Aspects of Modern Thought. Nine Sermons preached at St. Stephen's Church, Westbourne Park. With Preface by the Rev. Canon FARRAR. Crown 8vo. Cloth, price 5*s*.

SHAW (Major Wilkinson).

The Elements of Modern Tactics. Practically applied to English Formations. With Twenty-five Plates and Maps. Small crown 8vo. Cloth, price 12*s*.

*** The Second Volume of "Military Handbooks for Officers and Non-commissioned Officers." Edited by Lieut.-Col. C. B. Brackenbury, R.A., A.A.G.

SHAW (Flora L.).

Castle Blair: a Story of Youthful Lives. 2 vols. Crown 8vo. Cloth, gilt tops, price 12*s*. Also, an edition in one vol. Crown 8vo. 6*s*.

SHELLEY (Lady).

Shelley Memorials from Authentic Sources. With (now first printed) an Essay on Christianity by Percy Bysshe Shelley. With Portrait. Third Edition. Crown 8vo. Cloth, price 5*s*.

SHELLEY (Percy Bysshe).

Poems selected from. Dedicated to Lady Shelley. With Preface by Richard Garnett. Printed on hand-made paper. With miniature frontispiece. Elzevir. 8vo., limp parchment antique. Price 6*s*., vellum 7*s*. 6*d*.

SHERMAN (Gen. W. T.).

Memoirs of General W. T. Sherman, Commander of the Federal Forces in the American Civil War. By Himself. 2 vols. With Map. Demy 8vo Cloth, price 24*s*. *Copyright English Edition.*

SHILLITO (Rev. Joseph).

Womanhood: its Duties, Temptations, and Privileges. A Book for Young Women. Second Edition. Crown 8vo. Price 3*s*. 6*d*.

SHIPLEY (Rev. Orby), M.A.

Principles of the Faith in Relation to Sin. Topics for Thought in Times of Retreat. Eleven Addresses. With an Introduction on the neglect of Dogmatic Theology in the Church of England, and a Postscript on his leaving the Church of England. Demy 8vo. Cloth, price 12*s*.

Church Tracts, or Studies in Modern Problems. By various Writers. 2 vols. Crown 8vo. Cloth, price 5*s*. each.

SMITH (Edward), M.D., LL.B., F.R.S.

Health and Disease, as Influenced by the Daily, Seasonal, and other Cyclical Changes in the Human System. A New Edition. Post 8vo. Cloth, price 7*s*. 6*d*.

Foods. Profusely Illustrated. Sixth Edition. Crown 8vo. Cloth, price 5*s*.

Volume III. of The International Scientific Series.

SMITH (Edward), M.D., LL.B., F.R.S.—*continued.*

Practical Dietary for Families, Schools, and the Labouring Classes. A New Edition. Post 8vo. Cloth, price 3*s.* 6*d.*

Tubercular Consumption in its Early and Remediable Stages. Second Edition. Crown 8vo. Cloth, price 6*s.*

Songs of Two Worlds. By the Author of "The Epic of Hades." Fifth Edition. Complete in one Volume, with Portrait. Fcap. 8vo. Cloth, price 7*s.* 6*d.*

Songs for Music.
By Four Friends. Square crown 8vo. Cloth, price 5*s.*
Containing songs by Reginald A. Gatty, Stephen H. Gatty, Greville J. Chester, and Juliana Ewing.

SPEDDING (James).

Reviews and Discussions, Literary, Political, and Historical, not relating to Bacon. Demy 8vo. Cloth, price 12*s.* 6*d.*

SPENCER (Herbert).

The Study of Sociology. Eighth Edition. Crown 8vo. Cloth, price 5*s.*

Volume V. of The International Scientific Series.

STEDMAN (Edmund Clarence).

Lyrics and Idylls. With other Poems. Crown 8vo. Cloth, price 7*s.* 6*d.*

STEPHENS (Archibald John), LL.D.

The Folkestone Ritual Case. The Substance of the Argument delivered before the Judicial Committee of the Privy Council. On behalf of the Respondents. Demy 8vo. Cloth, price 6*s.*

STEVENS (William).

The Truce of God, and other Poems. Small crown 8vo. Cloth, price 3*s.* 6*d.*

STEVENSON (Robert Louis).

An Inland Voyage. With Frontispiece by Walter Crane. Crown 8vo. Cloth, price 7*s.* 6*d.*

STEVENSON (Robert Louis)—*continued.*

Travels with a Donkey in the Cevennes. With Frontispiece by Walter Crane. Crown 8vo. Cloth, price 7*s.* 6*d.*

STEVENSON (Rev. W. F.).

Hymns for the Church and Home. Selected and Edited by the Rev. W. Fleming Stevenson.

The most complete Hymn Book published.

The Hymn Book consists of Three Parts:—I. For Public Worship.—II. For Family and Private Worship.—III. For Children.

*** *Published in various forms and prices, the latter ranging from 8d. to 6s. Lists and full particulars will be furnished on application to the Publishers.*

STEWART (Prof. Balfour), M.A., LL.D., F.R.S.

On the Conservation of Energy. Fifth Edition. With Fourteen Engravings. Crown 8vo. Cloth, price 5*s.*

Volume VI. of The International Scientific Series.

STORR (Francis), and TURNER Hawes).

Canterbury Chimes; or, Chaucer Tales retold to Children. With Illustrations from the Ellesmere MS. Extra Fcap. 8vo. Cloth, price 3*s.* 6*d.*

STRETTON (Hesba).

David Lloyd's Last Will. With Four Illustrations. Royal 16mo., price 2*s.* 6*d.*

The Wonderful Life. Thirteenth Thousand. Fcap. 8vo. Cloth, price 2*s.* 6*d.*

Through a Needle's Eye: a Story. 2 vols. Crown 8vo. Cloth, gilt top, price 12*s.*

*** Also a Cheaper Edition in one volume, with Frontispiece. Crown 8vo. Cloth, price 6*s.*

STUBBS (Lieut.-Colonel F. W.)

The Regiment of Bengal Artillery. The History of its Organization, Equipment, and War Services. Compiled from Published Works, Official Records, and various Private Sources. With numerous Maps and Illustrations. 2 vols. Demy 8vo. Cloth, price 32*s.*

STUMM (Lieut. Hugo), German Military Attaché to the Khivan Expedition.

Russia's advance Eastward. Based on the Official Reports of. Translated by Capt. C. E. H. VINCENT. With Map. Crown 8vo. Cloth, price 6*s*.

SULLY (James), M.A.

Sensation and Intuition. Demy 8vo. Cloth, price 10*s*. 6*d*.

Pessimism: a History and a Criticism. Demy 8vo. Price 14*s*.

Sunnyland Stories. By the Author of "Aunt Mary's Bran Pie." Illustrated. Small 8vo. Cloth, price 3*s*. 6*d*.

Sweet Silvery Sayings of Shakespeare. Crown 8vo. Cloth gilt, price 7*s*. 6*d*.

SYME (David).

Outlines of an Industrial Science. Second Edition. Crown 8vo. Cloth, price 6*s*.

Tales from Ariosto. Retold for Children, by a Lady. With three illustrations. Crown 8vo. Cloth, price 4*s*. 6*d*.

TAYLOR (Algernon).

Guienne. Notes of an Autumn Tour. Crown 8vo. Cloth, price 4*s*. 6*d*.

TAYLOR (Sir H.).

Works Complete. Author's Edition, in 5 vols. Crown 8vo. Cloth, price 6*s*. each.

Vols. I. to III. containing the Poetical Works, Vols. IV. and V. the Prose Works.

TAYLOR (Col. Meadows), C.S.I., M.R.I.A.

A Noble Queen: a Romance of Indian History. Crown 8vo. Cloth. Price 6*s*.

Seeta. 3 vols. Crown 8vo. Cloth.

Tippoo Sultaun: a Tale of the Mysore War. New Edition with Frontispiece. Crown 8vo. Cloth, price 6*s*.

TAYLOR (Col. Meadows), C.S.I., M.R.I.A.—*continued.*

Ralph Darnell. New and Cheaper Edition. With Frontispiece. Crown 8vo. Cloth, price 6*s*.

The Confessions of a Thug. New Edition. Crown 8vo. Cloth, price 6*s*.

Tara: a Mahratta Tale. New Edition. Crown 8vo. Cloth, price 6*s*.

TEBBITT (Charles) and Francis Lloyd.

Extension of Empire Weakness? Deficits Ruin? With a Practical Scheme for the Reconstruction of Asiatic Turkey. Small crown 8vo. Cloth, price 3*s*. 6*d*.

TENNYSON (Alfred).

The Imperial Library Edition. Complete in 7 vols. Demy 8vo. Cloth, price £3 13*s*. 6*d*.; in Roxburgh binding, £4 7*s*. 6*d*.

Author's Edition. Complete in 6 Volumes. Post 8vo. Cloth gilt; or half-morocco, Roxburgh style:—

VOL. I. Early Poems, and English Idylls. Price 6*s*.; Roxburgh, 7*s*. 6*d*.

VOL. II. Locksley Hall, Lucretius, and other Poems. Price 6*s*.; Roxburgh, 7*s*. 6*d*.

VOL. III. The Idylls of the King (*Complete*). Price 7*s*. 6*d*.; Roxburgh, 9*s*.

VOL. IV. The Princess, and Maud. Price 6*s*.; Roxburgh, 7*s*. 6*d*.

VOL. V. Enoch Arden, and In Memoriam. Price 6*s*.; Roxburgh, 7*s*. 6*d*.

VOL. VI. Dramas. Price 7*s*.; Roxburgh, 8*s*. 6*d*.

Cabinet Edition. 12 vols. Each with Frontispiece. Fcap. 8vo. Cloth, price 2*s*. 6*d*. each.

CABINET EDITION. 12 vols. Complete in handsome Ornamental Case. 32*s*.

Pocket Volume Edition. 13 vols. In neat case, 36*s*. Ditto, ditto. Extra cloth gilt, in case, 42*s*.

TENNYSON (Alfred)—*continued.*

The Royal Edition. Complete in one vol. Cloth, 16*s.* Cloth extra, 18*s.* Roxburgh, half morocco, price 20*s.*

The Guinea Edition. Complete in 12 vols., neatly bound and enclosed in box. Cloth, price 21*s.* French morocco, price 31*s.* 6*d.*

The Shilling Edition of the Poetical and Dramatic Works, in 12 vols., pocket size. Price 1*s.* each.

The Crown Edition. Complete in one vol., strongly bound in cloth, price 6*s.* Cloth, extra gilt leaves, price 7*s.* 6*d.* Roxburgh, half morocco, price 8*s.* 6*d.*

*** Can also be had in a variety of other bindings.

Original Editions:

The Lover's Tale. (Now for the first time published.) Fcap. 8vo. Cloth, 3*s.* 6*d.*

Poems. Small 8vo. Cloth, price 6*s.*

Maud, and other Poems. Small 8vo. Cloth, price 3*s.* 6*d.*

The Princess. Small 8vo. Cloth, price 3*s.* 6*d.*

Idylls of the King. Small 8vo. Cloth, price 5*s.*

Idylls of the King. Complete. Small 8vo. Cloth, price 6*s.*

The Holy Grail, and other Poems. Small 8vo. Cloth, price 4*s.* 6*d.*

Gareth and Lynette. Small 8vo. Cloth, price 3*s.*

Enoch Arden, &c. Small 8vo. Cloth, price 3*s.* 6*d.*

In Memoriam. Small 8vo. Cloth, price 4*s.*

Queen Mary. A Drama. New Edition. Crown 8vo. Cloth, price 6*s.*

Harold. A Drama. Crown 8vo. Cloth, price 6*s.*

Selections from Tennyson's Works. Super royal 16mo. Cloth, price 3*s.* 6*d.* Cloth gilt extra, price 4*s.*

TENNYSON (Alfred)—*continued.*

Songs from Tennyson's Works. Super royal 16mo. Cloth extra, price 3*s.* 6*d.*

Also a cheap edition. 16mo. Cloth, price 2*s.* 6*d.*

Idylls of the King, and other Poems. Illustrated by Julia Margaret Cameron. 2 vols. Folio. Half-bound morocco, cloth sides, price £6 6*s.* each.

Tennyson for the Young and for Recitation. Specially arranged. Fcap. 8vo. Price 1*s.* 6*d.*

Tennyson Birthday Book. Edited by Emily Shakespear. 32mo. Cloth limp, 2*s.*; cloth extra, 3*s.*

*** A superior edition, printed in red and black, on antique paper, specially prepared. Small crown 8vo. Cloth extra, gilt leaves, price 5*s.*; and in various calf and morocco bindings.

In Memoriam. A new Edition, choicely printed on hand-made paper, with a Miniature Portrait in *eau forte* by Le Rat, after a photograph by the late Mrs. Cameron. Bound in limp parchment, antique, price 6*s.*, vellum 7*s.* 6*d.*

The Princess. A Medley. Choicely printed on hand-made paper, with a miniature frontispiece by H. M. Paget and a tail-piece in outline by Gordon Browne. Limp parchment, antique, price 6*s.*, vellum, price 7*s.*

Songs Set to Music, by various Composers. Edited by W. G. Cusins. Dedicated by express permission to Her Majesty the Queen. Royal 4to. Cloth extra, gilt leaves, price 21*s.*, or in half-morocco, price 25*s.*

THOMAS (Moy).

A Fight for Life. With Frontispiece. Crown 8vo. Cloth, price 3*s.* 6*d.*

THOMPSON (Alice C.).

Preludes. A Volume of Poems. Illustrated by Elizabeth Thompson (Painter of "The Roll Call"). 8vo. Cloth, price 7*s.* 6*d.*

THOMSON (J. Turnbull).
Social Problems; or, an Inquiry into the Law of Influences. With Diagrams. Demy 8vo. Cloth, price 10s. 6d.

THRING (Rev. Godfrey), B.A.
Hymns and Sacred Lyrics. Fcap. 8vo. Cloth, price 3s. 6d.

THURSTON (Prof. R. H.).
A History of the Growth of the Steam Engine. With numerous Illustrations. Second Edition. Crown 8vo. Cloth, price 6s. 6d.

TODHUNTER (Dr. J.)
A Study of Shelley. Crown 8vo. Cloth, price 7s.

Alcestis: A Dramatic Poem. Extra fcap. 8vo. Cloth, price 5s.

Laurella; and other Poems. Crown 8vo. Cloth, price 6s. 6d.

TOLINGSBY (Frere).
Elnora. An Indian Mythological Poem. Fcap. 8vo. Cloth, price 6s.

Translations from Dante, Petrarch, Michael Angelo, and Vittoria Colonna. Fcap. 8vo. Cloth, price 7s. 6d.

TURNER (Rev. C. Tennyson).
Sonnets, Lyrics, and Translations. Crown 8vo. Cloth, price 4s. 6d.

TWINING (Louisa).
Recollections of Workhouse Visiting and Management during twenty-five years. Small crown 8vo. Cloth, price 3s. 6d.

TYNDALL (John), LL.D., F.R.S
Forms of Water. A Familiar Exposition of the Origin and Phenomena of Glaciers. With Twenty-five Illustrations. Seventh Edition. Crown 8vo. Cloth, price 5s.
Volume I. of The International Scientific Series.

VAN BENEDEN (Mons.).
Animal Parasites and Messmates. With 83 Illustrations. Second Edition. Cloth, price 5s.
Volume XIX. of The International Scientific Series.

VAUGHAN (H. Halford), sometime Regius Professor of Modern History in Oxford University.
New Readings and Renderings of Shakespeare's Tragedies. Vol. I. Demy 8vo. Cloth, price 15s.

VILLARI (Prof.).
Niccolo Machiavelli and His Times. Translated by Linda Villari. 2 vols. Large post 8vo. Cloth, price 24s.

VINCENT (Capt. C. E. H.).
Elementary Military Geography, Reconnoitring, and Sketching. Compiled for Non-Commissioned Officers and Soldiers of all Arms. Square crown 8vo. Cloth, price 2s. 6d.

VOGEL (Dr. Hermann).
The Chemical Effects of Light and Photography, in their application to Art, Science, and Industry. The translation thoroughly revised. With 100 Illustrations, including some beautiful specimens of Photography. Third Edition. Crown 8vo. Cloth, price 5s.
Volume XV. of The International Scientific Series.

VYNER (Lady Mary).
Every day a Portion. Adapted from the Bible and the Prayer Book, for the Private Devotions of those living in Widowhood. Collected and edited by Lady Mary Vyner. Square crown 8vo. Cloth extra, price 5s.

WALDSTEIN (Charles), Ph. D.
The Balance of Emotion and Intellect: An Essay Introductory to the Study of Philosophy. Crown 8vo. Cloth, price 6s.

WALLER (Rev. C. B.)
The Apocalypse, Reviewed under the Light of the Doctrine of the Unfolding Ages and the Restitution of all Things. Demy 8vo. Cloth, price 12s.

WALTERS (Sophia Lydia).
The Brook: A Poem. Small crown 8vo. Cloth, price 3s. 6d.

WALTERS (Sophia Lydia)—*continued.*

A Dreamer's Sketch Book. With Twenty-one Illustrations by Percival Skelton, R. P. Leitch, W. H. J. Boot, and T. R. Pritchett. Engraved by J. D. Cooper. Fcap. 4to. Cloth, price 12*s.* 6*d.*

WARTENSLEBEN (Count H. von).

The Operations of the South Army in January and February, 1871. Compiled from the Official War Documents of the Head-quarters of the Southern Army. Translated by Colonel C. H. von Wright. With Maps. Demy 8vo. Cloth, price 6*s.*

The Operations of the First Army under Gen. von Manteuffel. Translated by Colonel C. H. von Wright. Uniform with the above. Demy 8vo. Cloth, price 9*s.*

WATERFIELD, W.

Hymns for Holy Days and Seasons. 32mo. Cloth, price 1*s.* 6*d.*

WATSON (William).

The Prince's Quest and other Poems. Crown 8vo. Cloth, price 5*s.*

WATSON (Sir Thomas), Bart., M.D.

The Abolition of Zymotic Diseases, and of other similar enemies of Mankind. Small crown 8vo. Cloth, price 3*s.* 6*d.*

WAY (A.), M.A.

The Odes of Horace Literally Translated in Metre. Fcap. 8vo. Cloth, price 2*s.*

WEBSTER (Augusta).

Disguises. A Drama. Small crown 8vo. Cloth, price 5*s.*

WEDMORE (Frederick).

The Masters of Genre Painting. With sixteen illustrations. Crown 8vo. Cloth, price 7*s.* 6*d*

WELLS (Capt. John C.), R.N.

Spitzbergen—The Gateway to the Polynia; or, A Voyage to Spitzbergen. With numerous Illustrations by Whymper and others, and Map. New and Cheaper Edition. Demy 8vo. Cloth, price 6*s.*

Wet Days, by a Farmer. Small crown 8vo. Cloth, price 6*s.*

WETMORE (W. S.).

Commercial Telegraphic Code. Second Edition. Post 4to. Boards, price 42*s.*

WHITAKER (Florence).

Christy's Inheritance. A London Story. Illustrated. Royal 16mo. Cloth, price 1*s.* 6*d.*

WHITE (A. D.), LL.D.

Warfare of Science. With Prefatory Note by Professor Tyndall. Second Edition. Crown 8vo. Cloth, price 3*s.* 6*d.*

WHITNEY (Prof. W. D.)

The Life and Growth of Language. Second Edition. Crown 8vo. Cloth, price 5*s.* *Copyright Edition.*

Volume XVI. of The International Scientific Series.

Essentials of English Grammar for the Use of Schools. Crown 8vo. Cloth, price 3*s.* 6*d.*

WICKHAM (Capt. E. H., R.A.)

Influence of Firearms upon Tactics: Historical and Critical Investigations. By an OFFICER OF SUPERIOR RANK (in the German Army). Translated by Captain E. H. Wickham, R.A. Demy 8vo. Cloth, price 7*s.* 6*d.*

WICKSTEED (P. H.).

Dante: Six Sermons. Crown 8vo. Cloth, price 5*s.*

WILLIAMS (Rowland), D.D.

Life and Letters of, with Extracts from his Note-Books. Edited by Mrs. Rowland Williams. With a Photographic Portrait. 2 vols. Large post 8vo. Cloth, price 24*s.*

Stray Thoughts from the Note-Books of the Late Rowland Williams, D.D. Edited by his Widow. Crown 8vo. Cloth, price 3*s.* 6*d.*

Psalms, Litanies, Counsels and Collects for Devout Persons. Edited by his Widow. New and Popular Edition. Crown 8vo. Cloth, price 3*s.* 6*d.*

WILLIS (R.), M.D.

Servetus and Calvin: a Study of an Important Epoch in the Early History of the Reformation. 8vo. Cloth, price 16*s*.

William Harvey. A History of the Discovery of the Circulation of the Blood. With a Portrait of Harvey, after Faithorne. Demy 8vo. Cloth, price 14*s*.

WILLOUGHBY (The Hon. Mrs.).

On the North Wind—Thistledown. A Volume of Poems. Elegantly bound. Small crown 8vo. Cloth, price 7*s*. 6*d*.

WILSON (H. Schütz).

The Tower and Scaffold. A Miniature Monograph. Large fcap. 8vo. Price 1*s*.

Within Sound of the Sea. By the Author of "Blue Roses," "Vera," &c. Third Edition. 2 vols. Crown 8vo. Cloth, gilt tops, price 12*s*.

*** Also a cheaper edition in one Vol. with frontispiece. Crown 8vo. Cloth, price 6*s*.

WOINOVITS (Capt. I.).

Austrian Cavalry Exercise. Translated by Captain W. S. Cooke. Crown 8vo. Cloth, price 7*s*.

WOLLSTONECRAFT (Mary).

Letters to Imlay. With a Preparatory Memoir by C. Kegan Paul, and two Portraits in *eau forte* by Anna Lea Merritt. Crown 8vo. Cloth, price 6*s*.

WOOD (Major-General J. Creighton).

Doubling the Consonant. Small crown 8vo. Cloth, price 1*s*. 6*d*.

WOODS (James Chapman).

A Child of the People, and other poems. Small crown 8vo. Cloth, price 5*s*.

WRIGHT (Rev. David), M.A.

Waiting for the Light, and other Sermons. Crown 8vo. Cloth, price 6*s*.

YOUMANS (Eliza A.).

An Essay on the Culture of the Observing Powers of Children, especially in connection with the Study of Botany. Edited, with Notes and a Supplement, by Joseph Payne, F.C.P., Author of "Lectures on the Science and Art of Education," &c. Crown 8vo. Cloth, price 2*s*. 6*d*.

First Book of Botany. Designed to Cultivate the Observing Powers of Children. With 300 Engravings. New and Cheaper Edition. Crown 8vo. Cloth, price 2*s*. 6*d*.

YOUMANS (Edward L.), M.D.

A Class Book of Chemistry, on the Basis of the New System. With 200 Illustrations. Crown 8vo. Cloth, price 5*s*.

YOUNG (William).

Gottlob, etcetera. Small crown 8vo. Cloth, price 3*s*. 6*d*.

ZIMMERN (H.).

Stories in Precious Stones. With Six Illustrations. Third Edition. Crown 8vo. Cloth, price 5*s*.